"Leadership at the Wheel: Navigating Your Route to Success"

(Master Key Leadership Skills Quickly and Confidently with Timeless Lessons from Route 17)

Quentin Walker

"Success is to be measured not so much by the position that one has reached in life as by the obstacles which he has overcome while trying to succeed."

– Booker T. Washington

Table of Contents

PREFACE

Leadership at the Wheel: Navigating Your Route to Success | Master Key Leadership Skills Quickly and Confidently with Timeless Lessons from Route 17

Imagine, for a moment, that you're embarking on a journey—not just any journey, but one that will define the essence of your career and shape the leader you aspire to become. This book is designed to be your companion on that voyage, offering both the map and the compass needed to navigate the often complex terrain of leadership.

My own leadership journey began long before I knew what leadership truly meant. It started when I was just six years old, riding the bus on Route 17. For most, the bus might seem like an ordinary way to get around, but for me, it became a classroom. That simple act of counting out twenty-five pennies for the fare each day taught me early lessons in resourcefulness, responsibility, and planning ahead. Each ride wasn't just a trip to a destination; it was a journey of observation, time management, and understanding the importance of making thoughtful choices.

As a six-year-old on Route 17, I began to notice things that would shape how I lead today. I observed people—how they interacted, how they handled conflict, and how some seemed to take charge while others followed. I learned the value of being aware of my surroundings and how important it was to navigate them with purpose. Without realizing it, these rides were my introduction to concepts that are central to leadership: self-awareness, decision-making, and accountability.

Those foundational lessons have stayed with me, evolving into principles that I now live by and teach others. Over the years, I've built on what I learned during those bus rides, refining my understanding of leadership and honing skills that help me navigate the challenges of leading people, teams, and organizations. But I also realized something else—many young leaders don't have those same foundational lessons to build upon.

This realization struck me vividly during a conversation with a young man after I had just given a presentation at my local Urban League. The presentation was on managing conflict, a skill many leaders struggle with. Afterwards, he approached me with thoughtful questions. He was ambitious, determined, and full of potential, but he felt stuck. He wanted to lead but didn't know where to start. The principles I had shared in the presentation resonated with him, and he expressed how much he wished someone had explained leadership in this way before.

That conversation was a turning point for me. It reminded me of the gap many young leaders face—not a gap in ambition but in guidance. Too many young professionals step into leadership roles without a roadmap. They're handed responsibility but not necessarily equipped with the tools to succeed. As a result, they struggle with accountability, communication, and building strong relationships—all critical components of effective leadership.

I started reflecting on the lessons I've learned over the years, from Route 17 to the boardroom. I thought about how those early rides taught me to take ownership of my choices, follow through on my commitments, and care for the people around me. I realized that these principles—follow-up, accountability, and care—are the cornerstones of leadership. They're not flashy or complicated, but they are essential. And they're the principles I want to share with you in this book.

Leadership at the Wheel is built on a straightforward yet powerful idea: great leadership starts with mastering the basics. Following up ensures that what needs to happen actually gets done. Accountability means taking responsibility for your actions and decisions, even when it's uncomfortable. Caring for the people you lead creates trust, loyalty, and a shared sense of purpose. These three pillars—follow-up, accountability, and care—are timeless, and they form the foundation of this book.

Each chapter is designed to be practical and actionable, blending personal stories with lessons I've learned from mentors, colleagues, and the leaders I admire most. You'll find relatable anecdotes, real-world examples, and strategies you can apply immediately, whether you're a college student stepping into your first leadership role, an early-career professional managing a team for the first time, or someone striving to refine your leadership skills in any setting.

For instance, in one chapter, we'll explore the importance of follow-up—not just as a way to track progress but as a tool for building trust and driving results. In another, we'll dive into accountability, discussing how owning your own decisions can create a culture where others feel empowered to do the same. And in yet another, we'll examine what it means to truly care for the people you lead, balancing compassion with the need to maintain high standards.

This book isn't about lofty theories or abstract ideas. It's about real leadership in the real world. It's about understanding that leadership isn't something you do alone—it's a responsibility to the people you lead and to yourself. It's about recognizing that the small, everyday actions—like following up on a promise, taking responsibility for a mistake, or simply listening—are what define great leaders.

I am deeply grateful to the mentors and colleagues who have shared their wisdom with me over the years. Their stories and insights have shaped my leadership philosophy and are woven throughout this book. I am also grateful to the young leaders who have inspired me with their passion and determination. Your questions and challenges have driven me to think more deeply about what it means to lead effectively, and this book is, in many ways, a response to you.

To you, the reader, thank you for choosing to invest in your growth as a leader. Whether you're just starting your journey or looking to sharpen your skills, this book is for you. My hope is that it will not only provide you with valuable tools but also inspire you to lead with integrity, purpose, and care.

As you turn each page, I encourage you to reflect on your own leadership journey. What lessons have you already learned, and where do you still need to grow? Leadership is not a destination—it's a process, a practice, and a commitment to becoming better every day. By the time you finish this book, I hope you'll feel more confident, more capable, and more inspired to lead in a way that leaves a lasting impact.

So, let's set forth together. Let's embrace the challenges and opportunities of leadership with open minds and eager hearts. Let's navigate the exciting, rewarding, and sometimes messy route to leadership success—together.

Sincerely,

Quentin J. Walker

Reflection for the Opening of Leadership at the Wheel: Navigating Your Route to Success

A bus stop sits on a corner I know well—where I spent countless mornings and afternoons as a child. Back then, it wasn't just a stop but a gateway. It represented movement, possibility, and often, necessity. This stop was where I learned patience, resourcefulness, and independence. I didn't know it then, but it was also where the foundation of my journey as a leader began.

Years later, I drove past that same corner in my dream car—a reflection of hard work, resilience, and the decisions that shaped my life. As I stopped to take a picture, the moment struck me deeply. In the glass of the bus stop shelter, I saw the car's reflection, a symbol of the progress I had made. It was a surreal intersection of my past and present, where the lessons of Route 17 met the rewards of perseverance and faith.

This image isn't just a snapshot; it's a story. It reminds us of the choices, sacrifices, and blessings that fueled the journey. Every late-night study session, every leap of faith, every tough decision—they all led to this moment. But more importantly, it's a testament to the power of vision and determination.

That bus stop taught me that every journey starts with showing up—whether waiting for the next ride or creating your own path. The reflection in that image is more than just a car; it's a reminder that with hard work, purpose, and the grace of opportunity, we can go from waiting for the bus to driving toward our dreams.

This book is rooted in the lessons from Route 17—the bus rides, the decisions, and the reflections that have guided my journey. I hope these stories and principles inspire you to navigate your own route to success with confidence and purpose, wherever your journey begins.

Chapter One

WHO HAS THE WHEEL?

Sitting at the head of a conference table at a nonprofit organization I support, I looked out at the young men gathered for the workshop I'd been invited to lead. Some leaned forward, eager to engage, while others sat back with crossed arms, skepticism written all over their faces. I knew that look—it was the same one I had years ago when I first questioned whether leadership was something you were born with or could learn.

Growing up, we didn't talk about leadership much at home. My assistant coach, a teammate's father, once said, "Some people are leaders, and some people are just players." I believed him for a long time. Some folks just seemed to naturally step up, while others stayed in the background. But as I grew older and started working, I began to wonder if that was the whole truth.

My first unofficial job was selling Christmas trees with my Boy Scout troop. We stood out in the cold for hours, hauling trees and learning how to talk to people. It was hard work, but it taught me the value of showing up and putting in the effort. Then came my first official job, working the cash register at a local movie theater. It wasn't glamorous, but it taught me discipline, responsibility, and how to deal with people from all walks of life.

I shared these stories with the group, watching as their expressions softened. "Leadership isn't about being born with it," I told them. "It's about the choices you make every day. It's about showing up, learning from your mistakes, and being willing to lift others up."

I noticed a shift in the room. The crossed arms relaxed, and a few started nodding. I could see the connection forming. Leadership wasn't some distant, unattainable thing. It was something they could build, step by step.

One of the young men raised his hand. "How do you deal with failure as a leader?" he asked.

I smiled. "You own it," I said. "Leadership isn't about being perfect—it's about being real. When you make a mistake, admit it. Learn from it. Show your team that it's okay to fail as long as you're growing."

By the end of the session, I could feel a change in the room. They weren't just listening anymore—they were reflecting, engaging, and starting to see themselves as leaders in their own lives. As they filed out, I stayed back, watching them go. Leadership isn't a destination, I thought. It's a journey. And for these young men, the journey had just begun.Leadership isn't about reaching a final destination—it's about the growth you embrace, the lessons you learn, and the impact you make along the way." – Quentin J. Walker

Can Leadership be Learned?

Unveiling the Myth of the Born Leader

Welcome to the journey of redefining leadership. It's a common misconception that leaders are just born that way—instinctively wise, assertive, and visionary from the cradle. This chapter starts by challenging this age-old belief, setting the stage for a transformative exploration into how true leadership is meticulously cultivated, not merely inherited.

Leadership, at its core, involves guiding others toward achieving shared goals, but it's much more than just taking charge—it's about vision, communication, and influencing team dynamics effectively. Let's delve into how these elements are not bestowed at birth but can be consciously developed through deliberate learning and experience.

Vision is the cornerstone of effective leadership. Without clarity of purpose, navigating through challenges becomes akin to sailing without a compass. This chapter will explore why having a clear and compelling vision is essential for any leader. We will examine how vision acts as a guiding star in decision-making processes and strategic planning.

Communication is another pivotal skill for any leader. It's not just about giving orders or making speeches; effective communication means ensuring your message resonates with your team, fostering an environment where ideas flow freely and everyone feels heard. We'll look at techniques that enhance your ability to communicate your vision and inspire your team to embrace it passionately.

Lastly, steering team dynamics effectively is crucial for turning plans into reality. Leadership involves more than just managing tasks; it's about nurturing a team culture that aligns with organizational goals and values. This chapter introduces strategies to master this art— turning potential conflicts into collaborative opportunities and aligning diverse talents towards common objectives.

As we unpack these themes, we'll weave in actionable insights from various leaders who started their journeys from scratch. They were not born with a leadership manual in hand; they learned, stumbled, and grew into their roles through experiences that shaped their capabilities over time.

This book promises not only to guide you through developing key leadership skills but also to empower you with the confidence to apply them effectively in your career. Whether you are stepping into a leadership role for the first time or looking to refine your skills further, this roadmap is designed to help you navigate with assurance and agility.

Remember, the transformation from being someone who leads to a leader who inspires is a journey of continuous learning and adaptation. By embracing the principles discussed here, you will be well-equipped to steer your team toward success—no matter what challenges lie ahead on the road.

Let's start this drive together, learning how to shift gears smoothly from foundational theories to practical applications in leadership. Get ready to dismantle old myths and discover how you can craft your own legacy of effective leadership through dedication and informed strategies.

Leadership begins with clarity. A leader's vision serves as the compass that guides their team toward a common goal. Without a clear vision, efforts can become scattered and unfocused, leading to frustration and disillusionment among team members. **Establishing a well-defined vision is not merely a task; it is an essential foundation upon which effective leadership is built.** It sets the tone for everything that follows, influencing decisions, actions, and the overall culture of the team.

To grasp the importance of having a clear vision, consider how it affects motivation. When leaders articulate their vision clearly, they ignite passion and commitment within their teams. People want to understand *why* they are doing what they do. A compelling vision provides that context and meaning. It helps individuals connect their roles to the larger picture, fostering a sense of purpose that drives engagement and productivity.

Moreover, a clear vision enables leaders to make informed decisions. Every choice—whether it's allocating resources or prioritizing tasks—can be measured against this guiding principle. For instance, when faced with multiple options, a leader can ask themselves: "Does this align with our vision?" If the answer is no, it becomes easier to set aside distractions and focus on what truly matters. This decisiveness not only aids in personal effectiveness but also instils confidence in team members who look to their leader for direction.

In addition to guiding decision-making, a well-articulated vision fosters unity among team members. Individuals may have diverse backgrounds and perspectives; however, when everyone shares a common objective, collaboration becomes more seamless. **A shared vision acts as a glue**, binding people together in pursuit of collective goals. This unity encourages open communication and fosters an environment where ideas can flourish, ultimately leading to innovative solutions.

Creating a clear vision isn't just about crafting lofty statements or slogans; it requires deep introspection and an understanding of core values and long-term aspirations. Leaders must reflect on what truly matters—not only to them but also to their teams and stakeholders. This process involves asking critical questions: What impact do we want to have? How do we envision our future? Engaging in this kind of reflective practice allows leaders to develop a meaningful vision that resonates at all levels.

Once established, the challenge shifts from creation to communication. A leader must effectively convey their vision so that it resonates with others. This involves using relatable language and demonstrating a genuine passion for the mission at hand. Storytelling can be particularly effective here—sharing personal experiences or anecdotes related to the vision can help others visualize its significance and relevance.

As leaders strive for clarity in their visions, it's essential they remain adaptable as circumstances evolve. The business landscape is dynamic; external factors may necessitate adjustments in strategy or focus while still aligning with the overarching vision. Being flexible does not mean compromising one's goals; rather, it reflects an understanding that **visionary leadership is also about navigating change thoughtfully** while keeping everyone aligned on shared values and objectives.

Are you ready to transform your communication skills for maximum impact?

The Heart of Communication

Effective communication is at the core of leadership. When you possess a clear vision, the next step is to share it with your team in a way that resonates. *Clarity and consistency* are essential; if your team doesn't understand your vision, they cannot align their efforts toward achieving it. It's not just about conveying information; it's about inspiring others to embrace that vision as their own.

To communicate effectively, you must first ensure that your message is clear and compelling. Avoid jargon or overly complex language. Instead, use simple and direct words that everyone can understand. A well-articulated message can ignite passion and commitment in your team members. Think about how you would explain your vision to someone unfamiliar with the subject—this mindset will guide you to speak plainly yet powerfully.

The Role of Listening

Communication is a two-way street. As much as you need to articulate your vision, you must also listen actively to your team's feedback and ideas. This approach not only fosters an environment of trust but also encourages open dialogue. When team members feel heard, they are more likely to engage with the vision you're presenting. *Active listening* shows respect for their perspectives and reinforces that their contributions matter.

Make it a habit to solicit feedback regularly. Ask questions that invite discussion rather than simply seeking affirmation of what you've said. This practice can help refine your vision based on valuable insights from your team, making it even more robust and inclusive.

Creating a Shared Narrative

Transforming a vision into something tangible requires weaving it into the fabric of daily operations and interactions within the team. One effective method is storytelling. By crafting a narrative around your vision, you create a context that makes it relatable and memorable. Share stories of past successes or challenges faced along similar paths—these narratives can serve as powerful motivators.

Encourage team members to share their stories related to the vision as well. This collective storytelling can build camaraderie and reinforce a sense of purpose among the group, reminding everyone why they are working together toward this common goal.

Consistency in Action

Once you've communicated your vision, it's crucial to back it up with consistent actions. Your behaviour should align with what you express verbally; otherwise, trust will erode quickly. If you advocate for innovation but resist change when new ideas arise, your credibility suffers. Demonstrating through action reinforces the message you've communicated.

Set clear expectations for how each team member contributes toward realizing the shared vision. Make these expectations visible through regular check-ins or progress reports so everyone knows where they stand in relation to the goals set forth.

Tools for Effective Execution

In addition to verbal communication, consider utilizing various tools that facilitate collaboration among team members. Platforms such as project management software or collaborative workspaces can streamline communication and ensure everyone remains aligned with the overarching goals.

Visual aids like charts or infographics can also help clarify complex ideas and keep the vision front-and-center during meetings or brainstorming sessions. These tools make it easier for everyone on the team to visualize their role within the larger framework of shared objectives.

Empowering Your Team

Empowerment is key when executing your vision effectively. Allow team members autonomy in how they approach their tasks while still holding them accountable for results. This balance fosters innovation and encourages individuals to take ownership of their contributions toward achieving common goals.

Recognize achievements along the way—celebrating milestones builds momentum and keeps spirits high as everyone works together toward fulfilling the overall mission.

Continuous Improvement

Finally, remember that executing a vision is not a one-time event; it's an ongoing process requiring adaptation and refinement over time. Regularly revisit and reassess both your communication strategies and execution methods to ensure they remain effective as circumstances change.

Encourage an atmosphere where feedback on these processes is welcomed—not just from leadership but from all levels within the organization. This commitment to continuous improvement strengthens both communication channels and execution practices over time, ultimately leading to greater success in achieving shared objectives.

By mastering these aspects of communication and execution, young leaders can foster an environment where visions come alive through collective effort—a vital component in navigating any path toward success.

V.E.C. Model: Vision, Execution, Communication

Leadership is fundamentally about guiding teams towards shared objectives. To achieve this, one must master the intricate dynamics of team interactions and steer them towards common goals. This involves a structured approach that revolves around three core components: Vision Articulation, Vision Communication, and Vision Execution. Together, these elements form the V.E.C. model, which serves as a powerful tool for leaders to create alignment within their teams.

Vision Articulation

The first step in mastering team dynamics is **Vision Articulation**. This process starts with identifying core values and understanding the organization's mission. A clear vision isn't just a statement; it's a beacon that guides every action within the team. Leaders must articulate strategic objectives that resonate with their team members' aspirations while aligning with organizational goals.

For example, when a leader articulates a vision of innovation and collaboration, they set the stage for a culture that embraces creativity and teamwork. By defining what success looks like, in specific terms, leaders provide clarity and direction, enabling team members to understand how their contributions fit into the broader picture.

Vision Communication

Once the vision is articulated, the next crucial component is **Vision Communication**. Effective communication strategies are vital for ensuring that all team members not only hear the vision but also internalize it. This involves employing storytelling techniques to make the vision relatable and engaging.

Active listening plays an equally important role here; it allows leaders to gauge how well their message resonates with others. When team members feel heard and valued during discussions about the vision, they are more likely to embrace it as their own. This fosters a sense of ownership among team members, which can lead to greater motivation and commitment.

Vision Execution

The final piece of the puzzle is **Vision Execution**. Having a vision is essential, but without actionable plans, it remains just words on paper. Leaders must establish clear roles and responsibilities that align with the articulated vision while creating actionable steps to realize it.

Regular checkpoints are critical in this phase; they allow teams to assess progress towards their goals and adapt strategies as necessary. For instance, if a project isn't meeting its milestones due to unforeseen challenges, leaders can pivot quickly by reassessing tasks or reallocating resources. This adaptive approach helps maintain momentum toward achieving common goals.

Interconnections Between Components

The components of the V.E.C. model do not operate in isolation; they are interconnected and mutually reinforcing. A well-articulated vision strengthens communication efforts because it provides context for conversations around goals and tasks. Conversely, effective communication enhances articulation—feedback from team members can help refine and clarify the vision further.

Execution ties everything together by translating ideas into action. When execution falters, it can impact both communication and articulation by eroding trust in leadership's ability to deliver on promises. Leaders who recognize these dynamics can create a more resilient team environment where adjustments can be made seamlessly.

Dynamics Over Time

As teams evolve over time or face new challenges, the V.E.C. model adapts accordingly. Feedback loops emerge within this framework—progress in execution informs future communication strategies while ongoing conversations enhance understanding of the vision itself.

This dynamism allows leaders to maintain equilibrium within their teams amidst changing circumstances or expectations. It also fosters stability by reinforcing shared values through continuous dialogue around vision and performance.

Practical Implications

In practical terms, adopting this model equips leaders with the tools needed for effective management of their teams' collective efforts toward achieving goals. Businesses that utilize this structured approach can foster deeper engagement among employees while enhancing overall performance levels.

For instance, companies that prioritize clear vision articulation often see higher employee satisfaction rates because individuals understand how their work contributes to larger objectives. This clarity leads to improved retention rates and productivity—key drivers of long-term success.

As you explore this model further, consider how you might implement these principles within your own leadership practice or organization. The opportunities for development in applying this framework are vast—ranging from refining your own communication skills to fostering stronger connections among your team members.

By embracing this structured approach to leadership dynamics, you pave the way for enhanced collaboration and shared success across all levels of your organization—a true testament to what effective leadership can achieve.

As we wrap up this initial journey into leadership, remember that the ability to guide a team effectively hinges on three critical pillars: **vision, communication**, and **team dynamics**. These are not innate gifts but skills that you can develop and refine. The belief that leaders are simply born is a myth that we've dismantled together. Leadership is an art crafted through deliberate practice, learning, and adaptation.

Starting with a **clear vision**, it's the beacon that guides your team through the complexities of their tasks and challenges. It's essential, as a leader, to not only have this vision but also to share it compellingly with your team. This ensures everyone is aligned and moving in the same direction.

Next, the power of **effective communication** cannot be

overstated. It's the bridge between misunderstanding and clarity, between division and unity. By mastering communication, you ensure that your vision is not just heard but understood and embraced. This involves not just talking but listening—truly hearing your team's feedback and integrating it into the collective strategy.

Lastly, **steering team dynamics** towards common goals is akin to navigating a ship through turbulent waters. It requires an understanding of each team member's strengths and how they can be best utilized towards achieving collective success. It's about fostering an environment where collaboration flourishes and where every member feels valued and motivated.

As we move forward in this book, each chapter will build on these foundational skills, offering you practical strategies and insights to enhance your leadership journey. You'll discover how to harness these skills not just in ideal conditions but especially when the going gets tough.

This is just the beginning. The road ahead is filled with opportunities for growth and learning. By embracing the lessons shared here, you're setting the stage for transformative leadership experiences that will not only elevate your career but also enrich the lives of those you lead.

So, keep turning the pages. There's much more to learn, and the potential for growth is immense. Each chapter promises to equip you with the knowledge and skills to navigate the ever-evolving landscape of leadership successfully. Let's continue this journey together with the confidence that every step taken is a step towards becoming a more effective, inspiring leader.

Chapter Two

HANDLE THE BALL OR PASS IT

When Does Guidance Become Control?

The hum of the office filled the air like white noise—a blend of ringing phones, the distant clatter of keyboards, and the occasional laugh breaking the monotony. I stood by the conference room door, watching my team as they worked, their focus glued to screens and scattered notes. Leadership felt different today. It wasn't just about making sure everything got done—it was about figuring out how to let them do it their way without stepping in too much.

My mind drifted back to my days on the football field, where every play required teamwork, strategy, and trust. As an offensive lineman, my role wasn't about making flashy moves or scoring touchdowns. It was about creating the space for others to succeed, knowing when to step up and when to let my teammates take the lead. I often think about how those lessons shaped the way I lead today.

That memory came flooding back as I watched one of my team members sitting at his desk. His face was a mixture of frustration and determination, the kind of look I knew too well. He was wrestling with a customer request, and it clearly wasn't going the way he wanted.

The easy thing to do would've been to swoop in, tell him exactly how to fix it, and move on. That's what I thought good leaders were supposed to do—step in, take over, and solve the problem.

But something stopped me.

Instead of charging in, I walked over, pulled up a chair next to him, and leaned in. "What's going on?" I asked, keeping my voice calm and curious.

He looked up, surprised. "I'm stuck on the customer's request. They want something out of scope, but I'm trying to find a way to deliver without overcommitting."

I nodded, letting him vent for a moment before asking, "What options have you thought about so far?"

He paused, then started listing his ideas. Some were good; others needed work. But I let him talk it through, asking questions here and there to nudge him in the right direction. Before long, he had a plan—a solution he came up with, not one I handed him.

As he went back to his work, his energy felt different. He was confident, not just in the solution but in himself.

Leadership isn't about having all the answers. It's about creating space for others to find their own.

It reminded me of a football drill we used to run during practice. Our coach called it "make the read." The idea was simple: the quarterback had to analyze the defense and decide whether to pass, run, or hand off the ball. It wasn't about executing a scripted play—it was about trusting the process, trusting your teammates, and making decisions in the moment.

Leadership is like that. It's knowing when to step in and when to step back. It's about recognizing that the goal isn't to control every move but to guide the team toward the win.

By the time the office began to clear out for the evening, I found myself standing by the window, watching the city lights blink on one by one. The day had been long but good.

My team member wasn't the only one who'd grown that afternoon. I had, too. I'd learned that leadership wasn't about doing it all myself—it was about empowering others, even if it meant watching them struggle for a moment.

The sky outside was streaked with orange and purple as the sun dipped behind the skyline. I thought about my football coach and how his lessons had shaped me, both on the field and off. He taught me what control looked like, but my team was teaching me what guidance could do.

As I grabbed my bag and headed out for the night, I smiled to myself. Leadership wasn't about holding the ball every time. Sometimes, the best thing you can do is pass it and let someone else take the shot.

"True leadership isn't about controlling every play; it's about trusting your team to make the read and empowering them to take the shot." – Quentin J. Walker

Steering, Not Dictating: The Art of Leadership in Motion

Leadership often conjures images of a commanding figure at the helm, dictating every move. But imagine a scenario where leadership is more like a seasoned navigator, subtly guiding a crew through uncharted waters with assurance and grace. This approach not only changes the trajectory of leadership but also amplifies the potential within each team member.

In today's fast-paced world, the ability to pivot between directing and delegating is crucial. Leaders who master this art not only propel their teams forward but also foster an environment ripe for innovation and growth. This chapter delves into the nuanced skills of deciding when to take charge and when to pass the baton—essential techniques for any leader aiming for long-term success.

Identifying Moments for Action vs. Delegation

The decision to intervene directly or to delegate is pivotal in leadership. Understanding the dynamics of your team, recognizing the strengths and weaknesses, and assessing the urgency and scope of tasks at hand are all factors that play into this decision. We will explore how to effectively gauge these situations and make choices that benefit both the leader's and the team's objectives.

Decision-Making for Collective Achievement

Decision-making isn't just about choosing the right path; it's about weaving through options in a way that aligns with your team's overall success. This involves not just foresight but also adaptability in approach—knowing when a directive style is necessary versus when a more democratic approach is beneficial. In this section, we'll dissect these strategies to enhance your decision-making toolkit.

Building Trust Through Balanced Leadership

At its core, leadership is less about exerting control and more about building trust. When team members feel valued and understood, they are more likely to invest fully in their roles and responsibilities. This chapter will highlight methods to strengthen trust through consistent, fair, and empathetic leadership practices that encourage collaboration and foster a robust workplace culture.

Effective leadership acts as both anchor and sail; it provides stability during turbulence but also allows for flexibility when exploring new avenues. By learning when to firmly handle situations or when to entrust tasks to others, leaders can create a dynamic that leverages everyone's best qualities.

Guidance rather than control—this mantra doesn't strip leaders of their power but instead enriches their role with depth and resonance that commands respect naturally rather than forcefully. Through cultivating decision-making acumen that prioritizes collective triumphs and nurturing reliance through balanced interactions, leaders can transform their approach from one of oversight to one of insightful mentorship.

Navigating these waters may seem daunting at first glance, but with careful consideration and strategic application of these principles, any leader can steer their team towards shared success with confidence and clarity. After all, true leadership effectiveness lies in the subtle art of knowing when to hold on tightly and when to let go gracefully.

Effective leadership requires the ability to discern when to take direct action and when to delegate responsibilities. This balance is essential in fostering a productive environment where everyone can thrive. **Recognizing your strengths and weaknesses** as a leader is crucial. If you find yourself constantly stepping in to handle tasks, it may signal a lack of trust in your team or an inability to assess their capabilities. On the other hand, if you're hesitant to take the reins when necessary, you risk leaving your team without direction.

Taking direct action should be reserved for situations that demand immediate attention or when critical decisions are on the line. For instance, if a project is veering off course due to unforeseen challenges, your intervention might be necessary to realign the team's focus and resources. However, it's equally important to empower your team members by giving them autonomy over their responsibilities. This not only boosts their confidence but also encourages them to develop problem-solving skills.

Delegation is an art form that involves understanding each team member's strengths and interests. **When you delegate tasks effectively**, you're not just offloading work; you're entrusting others with responsibilities that can lead to their growth. By doing this, you create opportunities for team members to showcase their talents and contribute meaningfully. In turn, this fosters a sense of ownership and accountability within the group.

To make informed decisions about delegation, consider the context of the task at hand. Is it something that requires specialized knowledge? If so, it might be wise to delegate it to someone with expertise in that area. Alternatively, if the task is routine or procedural, it can often be handed off to a less experienced member who will benefit from the experience. **Assessing the complexity of tasks** allows you to assign responsibilities more strategically.

Communication plays a pivotal role in both direct action and delegation. When taking charge of a situation, clear communication ensures that your team understands your vision and expectations. Conversely, when delegating tasks, it's vital to provide context so that team members grasp the importance of what they're working on. This clarity helps avoid confusion and empowers individuals to make decisions aligned with overall objectives.

Feedback loops are essential regardless of whether you're acting directly or delegating tasks. Regular check-ins allow you to gauge progress and address any issues before they escalate. This not only keeps projects on track but also demonstrates your commitment as a leader who cares about your team's success.

Finally, remember that leadership isn't about doing everything yourself; it's about *creating an environment* where everyone feels capable of contributing their best efforts. Balancing direct action with effective delegation builds trust and respect among your team members while enhancing overall productivity.

Are You Ready to Empower Your Team?

Prioritizing Team Success through Decision-Making

Effective decision-making is a cornerstone of successful leadership. **Leaders must recognize that every choice they make has an impact on the entire team.** This awareness shifts the focus from individual agendas to collective outcomes. When decisions are made with the team's success in mind, it fosters a culture of collaboration and inclusivity. This means involving team members in discussions, valuing their input, and considering their perspectives before making final choices. By doing so, leaders not only enhance team morale but also cultivate a sense of ownership among team members.

To prioritize team success, leaders should develop a structured approach to decision-making. **Start by identifying the problem clearly and gathering relevant information.** Engaging the team during this phase can provide insights that might not be visible from a singular viewpoint. Encourage open dialogue where everyone feels safe to voice opinions and ideas without judgment. This collaborative atmosphere not only enhances creativity but also builds trust within the group, laying a foundation for more effective teamwork.

Another critical aspect is evaluating options based on how they align with team goals. **When weighing alternatives, consider both short-term and long-term impacts on the group's objectives.** Leaders should ask themselves: Will this decision help us achieve our collective goals? How will it affect team dynamics? This reflective process ensures that decisions made today do not hinder progress tomorrow. It also reinforces the importance of being forward-thinking, encouraging teams to work together toward common aspirations rather than getting sidetracked by immediate concerns.

Moreover, it's essential for leaders to remain adaptable in their decision-making processes. The business landscape is constantly evolving, and what may seem like the right choice today could shift tomorrow. **Being flexible allows leaders to pivot when necessary while keeping team priorities at the forefront.** This adaptability can be communicated through regular check-ins with the team, ensuring everyone stays aligned with changing circumstances and remains engaged in the decision-making process.

Additionally, transparency plays a significant role in effective leadership. **When decisions are made openly, team members feel respected and valued.** Sharing the rationale behind choices fosters understanding and reduces resistance to change. It helps build a culture where feedback is welcomed and acted upon, leading to continuous improvement in how decisions are approached.

Leaders should also be aware of their own biases during decision-making. **Self-awareness is crucial; recognizing personal inclinations can prevent skewed judgments that might overlook important viewpoints within the team.** Actively seeking diverse perspectives not only enriches decision quality but also empowers individuals who may feel marginalized or unheard.

Finally, it's essential to reflect on past decisions regularly. **Encourage a culture of learning by discussing what worked and what didn't after implementing choices.** This practice allows teams to grow together, adapting based on shared experiences rather than isolated incidents. Emphasizing learning over blame helps maintain motivation and encourages innovative thinking moving forward.

In summary, developing decision-making skills that prioritize team success involves clarity, collaboration, adaptability, transparency, self-awareness, and reflection. By fostering these principles within your leadership style, you create an environment where every member feels empowered to contribute towards achieving common goals—ultimately steering your team toward greater success together.

Building Trust Through Transparency

Trust is the foundation of any successful team. Without it, communication breaks down, collaboration falters, and productivity suffers. As a leader, your responsibility is to create an environment where team members feel safe to express their ideas and concerns. This starts with **transparency**. Be open about your decisions and the reasons behind them. When your team understands the "why" of your actions, they are more likely to trust your judgment.

Encourage dialogue by inviting feedback on your leadership style and decisions. This isn't just about gathering opinions; it's about showing that you value input from every team member. Make it clear that their voices matter. By doing this, you foster a sense of ownership among your team members, which can significantly enhance their commitment to shared goals.

Balancing Authority and Approachability

Effective leadership requires a balance between being

authoritative and approachable. While it's essential to provide direction, it's equally important to be accessible. When team members perceive you as approachable, they are more likely to seek guidance when challenges arise rather than struggling in silence.

One way to achieve this balance is by **actively listening**. When someone approaches you with a problem or idea, give them your full attention. Make eye contact, nod in acknowledgement, and respond thoughtfully. This signals that you care about what they have to say, thus reinforcing their trust in you as a leader.

Empowering Others to Take Initiative

A significant aspect of building trust is empowering your team members to take initiative. When you delegate responsibilities effectively, you demonstrate confidence in their abilities. This not only boosts morale but also encourages them to take ownership of their work.

However, delegation should not mean stepping back entirely; it involves providing support while allowing individuals the freedom to make decisions. *This approach nurtures a culture of accountability,* where team members feel responsible for their tasks and are motivated to perform at their best.

Creating a Culture of Recognition

Acknowledging achievements—big or small—is vital for enhancing trust within your team. When you recognize individual contributions publicly or privately, it reinforces that hard work does not go unnoticed. This fosters an environment where people feel valued and appreciated.

Moreover, recognition should be specific. Instead of vague praise like "Good job," articulate what was done well—"Your presentation was thorough and engaging." This specificity shows that you are genuinely paying attention and can inspire others to strive for similar excellence.

Encouraging Collaboration Over Competition

Healthy competition can drive performance, but fostering collaboration within the team yields far greater benefits in terms of trust-building. Encourage team members to share resources and support one another rather than competing for recognition or rewards.

Implementing group projects or brainstorming sessions can facilitate collaborative efforts while building relationships among team members. When individuals learn to rely on each other's strengths, it creates a robust network of support that enhances overall trust in the group dynamic.

Maintaining Consistency in Leadership Style

Consistency is crucial in establishing trust as a leader. If your behaviour changes frequently or if you're unpredictable in how you handle situations, it can create confusion and anxiety among team members. Strive for consistency in how you communicate expectations and respond to challenges.

This doesn't mean being rigid; rather, it's about being reliable in your approach while adapting flexibly when needed. A consistent leadership style creates a predictable environment where team members know what to expect from you, leading them to feel secure in their roles.

Leading by Example

Your actions speak louder than words when it comes to building trust within your team. Demonstrate integrity by following through on commitments and admitting mistakes when they occur. This authenticity resonates with others and sets a standard for behaviour throughout the organization.

When leaders exhibit qualities such as transparency, accountability, and respect, they inspire similar behaviour among their teams. By leading by example, you create a culture where trust thrives naturally—encouraging everyone to contribute positively toward shared objectives.

In summary, enhancing trust within your team involves creating an open environment where communication flows freely, balancing authority with approachability, empowering others, recognizing achievements, fostering collaboration, maintaining consistency, and leading by example. As you develop these aspects of balanced leadership, you'll cultivate an atmosphere ripe for innovation and success—where every member feels valued and motivated towards common goals.

As we wrap up this discussion, let's reflect on the significant strides we've made together in understanding the delicate balance of leadership. **Effective leadership** is not about wielding control but about guiding and empowering those around us to achieve collective success. It's about knowing when to step forward and when to step back—allowing your team the space to grow, thrive, and contribute to shared goals.

Navigating Decisions: A Roadmap

Imagine you're at the helm of a ship. The vast ocean is your marketplace, full of tumultuous waves and unpredictable weather. Your crew looks to you; their trust in your decisions is paramount. Here's how you can steer confidently:

1. **Assess the Situation**: Take a comprehensive look at the current scenario. What are the tasks at hand? What resources are available? How critical are these tasks to your journey?

2. **Categorize Tasks**: Divide tasks into three distinct categories:

   ○ Critical tasks requiring your direct involvement

   ○ Tasks suitable for delegation

   ▪ Non-urgent tasks that can be postponed or dropped

3. **Match Tasks with Team Strengths**: Understand each crew member's strengths and weaknesses. Delegate accordingly, ensuring that everyone is in the right role to maximize their potential and contribution.

4. **Communicate Clearly**: When delegating, be clear about expectations and deadlines. This clarity will prevent misunderstandings and set clear benchmarks for success.

5. **Regular Check-ins**: Maintain a balance between oversight and autonomy. Regular updates can help keep the ship on course without oversteering.

6. **Reflect and Adapt**: Post-task, take time to reflect on what went well and what didn't. This reflection is crucial for continuous improvement and helps refine your decision-making skills over time.

By following these steps, you not only foster an environment of trust and accountability but also enhance the overall efficiency and morale of your team. Remember, a true leader doesn't just sail the ship—they empower their crew to navigate through the roughest waters.

Leadership, at its core, is an ongoing journey of self-improvement and adaptation. It requires a keen understanding of when to take the wheel and when to pass it on. By mastering this balance, you ensure that your team is not just following directions but actively engaging in the route to success. This not only leads to better outcomes but also fosters a culture of respect and mutual growth.

In our next chapter, we will delve deeper into understanding and cultivating the resilience needed to withstand the storms you'll inevitably face on this voyage. As you continue to navigate your leadership journey, keep refining these skills—they are your compass in the ever-changing tides of professional landscapes.

Chapter Three

SAY IT STRAIGHT

The sun wasn't even up yet as I stood waiting for the train to the airport terminal. The platform was quiet except for the occasional rustle of newspapers and the distant hum of a coffee machine. My mind wasn't on the early morning chill, though; it was on a looming business decision. It is one of those choices that could either propel the company forward or derail months of hard work. These were the moments where clarity mattered most, and the best way to find it, I've learned, is by cutting through the noise and saying it straight.

As I waited, a memory surfaced, pulling me back to my childhood rides on Route 17. Back then, I didn't realize those rides would teach me as much as they did. As a boy, I would count my pennies carefully, knowing that if I spent too much on the ride to my destination, I might not have enough to get back. The stakes weren't high in the grand scheme of things, but for a six-year-old, they were everything. Every decision had to be deliberate, and every plan was precise. And when it wasn't, I quickly learned the cost of misjudgment.

Leadership is a lot like those early bus rides. It's about understanding what's essential, anticipating what might come next, and making decisions with the resources you have. But above all, it's about communicating those decisions clearly—both to yourself and to those you're leading. There's no room for ambiguity when others are counting on you to guide the way.

I boarded the train, the low hum of its movement pulling me out of my thoughts for a moment. Across from me sat a man in his mid-forties, scrolling on his phone with a look of quiet intensity. I've seen that look before—on colleagues, team members, and even in the mirror. It's the expression of someone trying to make sense of a problem. I wondered briefly what was on his mind. Maybe it was a deal gone sideways, a looming deadline, or a conversation he was dreading. Whatever it was, I hoped he'd approach it with honesty because I've learned there's no other way.

Years ago, early in my career, I found myself in a situation where I didn't say it straight. I danced around the truth, thinking I was sparing someone's feelings, avoiding conflict, or maybe just trying to buy time. It didn't work. The lack of clarity caused confusion, delays, and frustration—both for me and for the people I was leading. I learned the hard way that sugarcoating or sidestepping only creates bigger problems down the line. Clarity is kindness. Honesty, even when it's uncomfortable, is respect.

As the train swayed along its path, I thought about the young man I'd mentored a few months ago. He was new to leadership, full of ideas, but hesitant to make tough calls. "What if I make the wrong decision?" he asked me one day. I told him what I wish someone had told me early on: "You're going to make wrong decisions. That's inevitable. But what will matter most is how you own them and communicate them. People can work with mistakes. They can't work with uncertainty."

The train came to a stop, and a young mother stepped on, juggling a stroller and a toddler while trying to find a seat. As the doors closed behind her, the toddler dropped a toy, and it rolled toward me. I picked it up and handed it back, offering a smile. She thanked me with an apologetic look as if she'd disrupted my day, but she hadn't. Leadership often feels like this moment—balancing your own responsibilities while being present enough to help someone else. And sometimes, those small gestures of care say more than any words ever could.

I stared out the window as the city began to wake up, its skyline reflecting the first light of day. Leadership is a balancing act between decisiveness and empathy, between saying it straight and saying it in a way people can hear. It's not just about what you say but how you say it. The truth was delivered poorly, and it can still land like a punch. But the same truth, delivered with care and intention, can build trust, inspire action, and move people forward.

By the time I reached the terminal, my thoughts were clearer. The decision I had been agonizing over didn't seem so daunting anymore. I knew what needed to be done, and I knew how to say it. It wasn't going to be easy, but that wasn't the point. Leadership isn't about taking the easy way out. It's about showing up, being honest, and trusting that the people around you will rise to meet the moment if you give them the tools and clarity they need.

As I walked through the terminal, I thought again about those rides on Route 17. Back then, I had to be clear with myself: Did I have enough money for the return trip? Did I know where to get off? Was I ready to make the walk home if things didn't go as planned? Those small moments of clarity, of saying it straight to myself, laid the foundation for how I approach leadership today. The stakes are higher now, and the decisions are more complex, but the principle is the same.

Say it straight, not just to others but to yourself. Be honest about what you know and what you don't. Be clear about what needs to happen and why. And most importantly, trust that clarity, even when it's uncomfortable, will always lead to better outcomes than avoiding the truth.

That morning, as I boarded the plane, I felt a renewed sense of purpose. Leadership is a journey, one that requires constant learning, reflection, and growth. But above all, it requires clarity. Because when you say it straight, you give yourself and those you lead the best chance to succeed.

A Childhood Experiences Shape a Leader?

"Clarity is the cornerstone of leadership—it cuts through uncertainty, builds trust, and paves the way for action. Say it straight, to others and yourself, because avoiding the truth only delays the growth you and your team deserve." – Quentin J. Walker

From Route 17 to Boardroom Brilliance

When you think back to your first lessons in leadership, your mind might not immediately recall the hum of a bus engine or the jostling seats of public transport. Yet, it's in these everyday experiences that foundational skills can begin to take shape. As we delve into the heart of leadership, it's essential to recognize that clear, honest communication isn't just a soft skill—it's the cornerstone upon which trust is built within any successful team.

Picture yourself navigating a complex bus route as a child. The challenge wasn't just about getting from point A to B; it was about understanding the timetable, managing your fare, and deciding when and where to get off. These early lessons in resource management and accountability are direct parallels to essential leadership skills. They underscore a profound truth: our formative experiences profoundly shape how we lead.

The Power of Clarity

To foster an environment where trust thrives and teams can flourish, **leaders must prioritize transparency**. This chapter will explore why the clarity of your message can be as critical as the message itself. Just as a bus route announces each stop clearly to avoid confusion, a leader must communicate goals and expectations with equal clarity. This not only sets the stage for mutual understanding but also aligns team efforts harmoniously.

Strategies for Misunderstanding-Free Communication

Misunderstandings can derail even the most well-intentioned projects faster than unexpected roadblocks on Route 17. In this discussion, we'll introduce practical strategies designed to keep communication lines open and clear. Implementing these tactics effectively can be likened to ensuring all passengers on a bus know their stops; it's about making sure everyone is on the same page and prepared for what's ahead.

Cultivating Conversational Highways

Encouraging open dialogue is akin to opening more lanes on a highway; it allows for smoother, faster travel in which ideas can flow freely without congestion. This chapter will highlight how fostering an environment that values each team member's input leads to more innovative solutions and a more agile response to challenges.

By examining these key aspects of communication within leadership, you'll gain insights into how seemingly simple principles can translate into powerful tools for leading any team towards success. Each section is designed not only to inform but also to equip you with actionable strategies that you can apply directly to your leadership practice.

Remember, effective leadership is less about commanding from high above and more about navigating alongside your team—much like everyone sharing a journey on Route 17. Here, every lesson learned adds another layer of depth to your leadership abilities, preparing you for whatever lies ahead on your route to success.

So, let's embark on this journey together—tackling each challenge as an opportunity to enhance our skills and lead with confidence and clarity.

Clear and honest communication forms the cornerstone of effective leadership. When leaders communicate openly, they foster an environment of trust where team members feel valued and understood. This is not just about being straightforward; it's about ensuring that your message is received accurately and with the right intention. If your team senses that you are being transparent, they are more likely to reciprocate with honesty in their own interactions.

Building trust through communication requires a commitment to clarity. When you articulate your expectations and vision clearly, you eliminate ambiguity that can lead to confusion. Ambiguity can breed misunderstandings, which in turn can erode trust. For instance, if a leader communicates a project deadline without explaining the rationale behind it, team members might question its importance or feasibility. By providing context, leaders help their teams understand the bigger picture and how their roles contribute to it.

It's also crucial to practice active listening. Communication is a two-way street, and listening effectively allows leaders to gauge the sentiments and concerns of their team. When individuals feel heard, they are more likely to share their ideas and feedback openly. This creates a culture where team members feel safe expressing themselves without fear of judgment or repercussions. As a leader, make it a habit to ask questions that invite discussion rather than simply delivering instructions.

Moreover, non-verbal cues play an essential role in communication. Your body language, eye contact, and tone of voice can either reinforce or undermine your message. For example, if you're discussing important changes while appearing distracted or disengaged, your team may interpret this as a lack of investment in their success. Being mindful of how you present yourself physically can enhance the clarity of your verbal messages.

In situations where difficult conversations are necessary—be it addressing performance issues or project setbacks—approach these discussions with transparency and empathy. Acknowledging challenges openly while focusing on solutions builds credibility as a leader. When team members see that you are willing to confront problems head-on rather than gloss over them, they are more likely to trust your leadership during turbulent times.

Creating an atmosphere of open communication is not solely about sharing information; it also involves encouraging feedback from your team. Regular check-ins provide opportunities for team members to express their thoughts on processes or issues they face in their roles. By valuing their input, you not only demonstrate respect but also position yourself as a leader who is approachable and invested in the team's well-being.

Finally, remember that clear communication should be consistent across all levels of leadership within an organization. If messages from different leaders conflict or lack coherence, it can lead to distrust among employees regarding who they should turn to for guidance or support. Establishing unified communication channels ensures everyone is aligned towards common goals.

As you reflect on your communication style and its impact on building trust within your team, consider how small adjustments can yield significant improvements in overall morale and productivity.

Ready for More Insights?

Clarity as a Cornerstone

Effective communication is the bedrock of any successful team. When leaders articulate their expectations clearly, they create an environment where misunderstandings are minimized. This clarity allows team members to focus on their tasks rather than navigating unclear directives. **Establishing a straightforward communication style can dramatically improve the overall efficiency and morale of the team.** It's not just about what is said but how it's conveyed.

One effective strategy is to employ *active listening*. This means truly engaging with what others are saying, not merely waiting for your turn to speak. When team members feel heard, they are more likely to express their thoughts openly. A simple nod or verbal affirmation can go a long way in fostering an atmosphere where people feel comfortable sharing their ideas and concerns. **By practising active listening, leaders can catch potential misunderstandings before they escalate into larger issues.**

Another important approach is to **encourage feedback** at every level of communication. When feedback becomes a norm, it creates a culture of transparency. Leaders should actively seek input from their team members on projects and decisions. This not only clarifies expectations but also empowers individuals to voice their insights or raise concerns early on. Creating channels for feedback—whether through regular check-ins or anonymous surveys—can prevent small misunderstandings from developing into major setbacks.

Simplicity in Communication

Complex language can often lead to confusion and misinterpretation. Leaders should strive for simplicity in their communication style. Using clear, concise language ensures that messages are easily understood by everyone involved, regardless of their background or expertise. **Avoid jargon and technical terms unless absolutely necessary; always consider the audience's perspective when conveying information.** Simplifying communication does not mean sacrificing depth; instead, it means being intentional about clarity.

Visual aids can also enhance understanding. Diagrams, charts, or even simple bullet points can break down complex information into digestible pieces. *When people can visualize information*, it becomes easier for them to grasp key concepts and retain details. Leaders who leverage visual tools often find that their teams have fewer questions and better comprehension of tasks at hand.

Consistency Builds Trust

Consistency in messaging reinforces trust among team members. When leaders communicate regularly and reliably, they set a standard for accountability that resonates throughout the organization. **This consistency helps establish a rhythm where everyone knows what to expect**, reducing anxiety around changes or decisions that may arise unexpectedly.

Creating a structured communication schedule—like weekly

updates or daily stand-ups—can be beneficial in maintaining this consistency. Such routines create opportunities for everyone to stay aligned on goals and tasks while also providing a platform for addressing any emerging issues promptly.

Anticipating Questions

Leaders should not only communicate what needs to be done but also anticipate questions that might arise from their instructions. This proactive approach shows foresight and consideration for the team's needs, which builds confidence in leadership decisions. By providing context and rationale behind decisions, leaders enable team members to understand the bigger picture and make informed choices themselves.

Creating FAQ documents or hosting Q&A sessions following major announcements can help clarify uncertainties right away. This practice encourages engagement and demonstrates that leadership values input from all levels.

Emphasizing Non-Verbal Cues

Lastly, it's essential to recognize the role of non-verbal communication in conveying messages effectively. Body language, tone of voice, and facial expressions can significantly impact how words are interpreted by others. Being mindful of these cues ensures that leaders project openness and approachability.

For instance, maintaining eye contact during conversations signals attentiveness and respect for the speaker's input. Similarly, using an inviting tone encourages others to share their thoughts without fear of judgment or dismissal.

By implementing these strategies—clarity in messaging, active listening, encouraging feedback, simplicity in language, consistency in communications, anticipating questions, and being aware of nonverbal cues—leaders will not only reduce misunderstandings but also create an environment conducive to collaboration and innovation among their teams.

As young leaders navigate their paths forward, mastering these communication strategies will equip them with essential skills needed to foster teamwork and drive success within their organizations moving forward.

CLEAR MODEL OF COMMUNICATION

Effective communication is the backbone of any successful leadership approach. This model focuses on five key components: Clarity, Consistency, Openness, Feedback, and Nonverbal Communication. Each element plays a critical role in facilitating open dialogue and fostering a collaborative team environment.

Clarity

Clarity is essential in communication. When messages are articulated in straightforward language, they eliminate ambiguity and confusion. **Leaders must strive to express their thoughts clearly** to ensure everyone understands their intentions and objectives. This clarity enables team members to align their efforts with the leader's vision and enhances overall productivity. A lack of clarity can lead to misunderstandings, which can disrupt teamwork and hinder progress.

Consistency

Consistency reinforces trust within a team. When leaders communicate the same message across various platforms—be it meetings, emails, or casual conversations—**it builds reliability**. Team members begin to feel secure knowing that they can expect the same information regardless of the context. This consistency not only strengthens relationships but also ensures that everyone is on the same page, reducing the chances of conflict or misinterpretation.

Openness

Creating an atmosphere of openness is crucial for encouraging dialogue. Leaders should actively promote environments where team members feel comfortable expressing their ideas, questions, and concerns. **This openness invites collaboration** and fosters innovation, as individuals are more likely to share creative solutions when they feel heard and valued. Open dialogue also helps identify potential issues before they escalate into larger problems.

Feedback

Feedback is a two-way street essential for effective communication. Leaders should not only provide guidance but also encourage input from their team members. **Constructive feedback allows for growth**, both individually and collectively. When team members feel their opinions matter, it nurtures a sense of ownership over projects and tasks. Regular feedback sessions contribute to continuous improvement while reinforcing the importance of every individual's contributions.

Nonverbal Communication

Nonverbal cues play a significant role in how messages are received. Body language, tone of voice, and facial expressions can either enhance or undermine verbal communication. **Leaders must be aware of these nonverbal signals**, as they often convey more than words alone. Being mindful of nonverbal communication fosters an atmosphere of trust and respect while allowing leaders to better understand their team's sentiments.

The interplay between these components forms a robust framework that supports effective communication in leadership roles. When clarity aligns with consistency, it establishes a foundation upon which openness can thrive. Openness invites feedback, creating a cycle that promotes ongoing dialogue and innovation within teams.

Over time, this model adapts to various conditions within the workplace environment. For instance, during periods of change or uncertainty, maintaining clarity becomes even more vital to prevent confusion among team members. The feedback loop ensures that leaders remain attuned to their team's needs while reinforcing trust through consistent messaging.

The practical implications of this model are significant for organizations aiming to achieve their goals effectively. By fostering an environment rooted in clear communication, teams become more cohesive and responsive to challenges. This approach not only enhances productivity but also contributes to employee satisfaction, as individuals feel valued and understood.

In summary, incorporating these five elements into everyday leadership practices lays the groundwork for a collaborative culture where open dialogue flourishes. Future opportunities may arise from further exploring each component's nuances or adapting the model to suit different organizational contexts or leadership styles. By investing in effective communication strategies today, leaders can navigate toward success with greater confidence tomorrow.

Cultivating Clarity and Trust

Clear and honest communication isn't just a tool; it's the foundation of trust within a team. Imagine the difference in a team where every member speaks openly, with transparency and integrity. This approach not only builds trust but also strengthens the bonds within the team, making every project more manageable and every challenge less daunting.

Strategies to Steer Clear of Misunderstandings

Misunderstandings can derail even the most well-intentioned projects. By implementing effective communication strategies, you effectively set up guardrails that keep your team's conversations on track. Think of it as preventive maintenance for your team's dynamics; it's about ensuring smooth operations before any issues arise.

Encouraging Open Dialogue

Open dialogue is akin to opening the windows in a stuffy room—it revitalizes and invigorates. It encourages a flow of ideas, which fosters creativity and innovation. When team members feel confident in sharing their thoughts and opinions, they contribute more actively to the team's objectives, driving collective success.

The Route to Effective Leadership

Remember, the skills discussed here aren't just techniques; they are essential components of your leadership journey. Just like navigating a familiar route, these communication skills become second nature with practice and dedication. They are pivotal in steering your team towards success, making every interaction count, and ensuring that your leadership journey is as impactful as it is inspiring.

Embrace these practices with the commitment of a seasoned driver on a well-known road, knowing that each conversation, each open dialogue, and each strategy for clarity you implement moves you and your team closer to your shared goals.

Chapter Four

EVERYONE CAN'T COME TO THE BBQ

The weight of leadership doesn't just appear overnight; it builds slowly, growing heavier with every decision, every team meeting, and every person who depends on you to get it right. I learned that lesson early in my career, but the roots of that realization go even further back to a time when I had to figure out that not everyone is meant to come along for the journey.

It was a crisp spring morning, and I found myself coaching a young professional named Emmett. We met at a coffee shop downtown, tucked into a corner table near the window. The sunlight streaming through the glass illuminated his face, but it didn't erase the weariness in his eyes. He stirred his coffee absentmindedly, the faint clinking of the spoon against the cup almost drowning out his words.

Emmett was one of those people you could tell was built for leadership. He had that sharp focus, the hunger to succeed, and a natural ability to inspire others. But right now, all of that seemed buried beneath doubt.

"I don't get it," he said, shaking his head. "I thought building a team meant keeping everyone together, like a family. But it feels like I'm dragging people along who don't even want to be there."

That hit home. I've been there. And if you've ever tried to lead, I bet you've been there too.

I took a sip of my own coffee—black, no sugar, just the way I like it—and leaned forward. "Let me ask you something, Emmett. Have you ever planned a barbecue?"

He looked up, confused, but nodded. "Sure."

"And did you invite everyone you know?"

"No," he replied slowly. "I mean, I invited people I thought would actually show up and enjoy it."

"Exactly," I said, setting my cup down. "The same applies to leadership. Not everyone can come to the BBQ. Some people don't want to be there. Others won't bring anything to the table. And a few will show up just to complain that the food isn't good enough. You need to figure out who's worth inviting and who isn't."

He laughed at that, but I could see it was starting to click.

When I first started leading teams, I made the mistake of thinking I had to keep everyone happy, no matter what. I thought that if I could just find the right words or work hard enough, I could turn everyone into a high performer. It took me a long time to learn that leadership isn't about dragging people along who don't want to move. It's about surrounding yourself with people who are ready to grow, contribute, and bring their best.

Emmett sat quietly, mulling that over. "But what about the

ones who aren't ready? Or the ones who are just... difficult?"

I smiled. "Sometimes, leadership means letting people go. Not because you don't care, but because holding onto them does more harm than good—for you, for the team, and even for them."

I thought back to one of my first big leadership lessons. I was in charge of a team at a time when we were going through a major transition. There was one guy on my team—I'll call him Vlad—who had been there longer than anyone else. He knew the business inside and out, but he resisted every change we tried to make. No matter how much I tried to coach him or get him on board, it was like hitting a brick wall.

For months, I told myself that if I just worked harder, I could win him over. I spent hours in one-on-ones and tried every motivational tactic I knew, but nothing worked. The truth was that Vlad wasn't willing to grow, and his resistance was holding the entire team back.

It wasn't easy, but I eventually had to make the call to let him go. And you know what happened? The team thrived. Without that constant friction, we were able to move forward, and Vlad found a role elsewhere where he was happier.

Leadership is about making those tough calls. It's about recognizing that not everyone is meant to be part of your journey—and that's okay.

Emmett looked out the window, watching the stream of people passing by. "I guess I've been trying to carry everyone with me, even the ones who don't want to move."

"And that's a heavy load to carry," I said. "Too heavy. You'll burn out if you try to be everything for everyone."

He nodded slowly, the tension in his shoulders easing just a bit.

"Here's the thing, Emmett. Leadership isn't just about the decisions you make—it's about the people you choose to bring along for the ride. The ones who show up ready to contribute, who want to be there, and who make the whole thing better just by being part of it. Those are the people worth investing in."

As we finished our coffee and stepped outside into the crisp morning air, I could see a shift in Emmett. The doubt was still there, but it was quieter now, replaced by something stronger: clarity.

Not everyone can come to the BBQ, and that's a good thing. Because when you surround yourself with the right people— those who bring value, energy, and a shared vision—everything else falls into place.

"Leadership isn't about carrying everyone; it's about choosing who's ready to move forward. The right team transforms effort into momentum." – Quentin J. Walker

Who Gets a Seat at Your Table?

Navigating the uncharted waters of leadership as a young professional can be as thrilling as it is daunting. Stepping into a leadership role often means facing a barrage of decisions that can shape not only your career but also the culture and success of your organization. Particularly for those newly appointed to leadership, the challenge is not just in making decisions but in making informed, effective decisions with limited experience to draw upon.

The Art of Team Selection

One of the first and most pivotal tasks you'll encounter as a leader is assembling your team. It's about **finding the right mix of skills, personalities, and work ethics** that align with your organization's culture and goals. Think of this process as curating rather than simply filling positions. You're not just looking for qualified individuals; you're looking for the right fit—a concept that will be explored deeply in this chapter.

Making the Tough Calls

Decision-making can feel like walking a tightrope. On one side, there's the pressure to maintain harmony within your team; on the other, the need to achieve aggressive organizational goals. This chapter will delve into why embracing the discomfort of tough decision-making can be a transformative experience for young leaders. It's about understanding that some decisions, while difficult, are necessary for the health and growth of the team.

Dynamics That Drive Success

Once your team is assembled, managing its dynamics becomes your next critical focus. The ability to foster a productive working environment is pivotal. This involves more than just overseeing project deadlines or mediating conflicts; it's about nurturing an atmosphere where diverse ideas and personalities can collaborate effectively. We'll look at strategies to help you cultivate such an environment, ensuring that every team member can thrive and contribute to their fullest potential.

The journey of leadership is continuous and ever-evolving. For young leaders, this path is dotted with unique challenges that call for tailored guidance and insights. By focusing on these foundational aspects—selecting the right team members, making courageous decisions, and managing team dynamics—you set the stage not only for individual success but for crafting a resilient, adaptive team.

In this conversation about leadership, remember that while everyone may bring something to the table, not everyone will be right for your specific feast. The wisdom lies in knowing who to invite and how to align their strengths with your vision for success.

Through practical advice and relatable examples, this chapter aims not only to guide but also to inspire you to embrace these challenges with confidence and foresight. Here's to your journey to becoming a leader who doesn't just fill roles but fosters potential and drives innovation.

Selecting the right team members is crucial for any leader, especially for young leaders who are just starting their journey. The initial step in building a successful team is understanding the **core values and goals** of your organization. These elements serve as a compass that guides every decision you make regarding your team composition. When you know what your organization stands for, you can identify individuals whose values align with yours. This alignment fosters a cohesive work environment where everyone is on the same page, increasing both morale and productivity.

When evaluating potential team members, consider not only their skills and experience but also how they fit into the organizational culture. A talented individual may shine on paper, but if they clash with the team's values or dynamics, their contributions can become counterproductive. Look for candidates who exhibit traits that resonate with your organizational ethos—traits like collaboration, adaptability, and integrity. These characteristics often lead to stronger relationships within the team and can help mitigate conflicts down the line.

It's also essential to recognize that diverse teams bring unique perspectives to the table. By intentionally selecting members from various backgrounds, experiences, and viewpoints, you create an environment ripe for innovation and creativity. Different perspectives can challenge the status quo and inspire fresh ideas that propel your organization forward. However, diversity must be balanced with unity; ensuring that each member shares a commitment to common goals is vital.

The interview process offers a unique opportunity to gauge alignment with culture and goals. Instead of solely focusing on technical skills during interviews, ask behavioral questions that reveal how candidates have acted in previous situations. For example, inquire about times they faced challenges working in teams or how they contributed to a collective goal. Their responses will provide insight into whether they possess the collaborative spirit necessary for your organization.

Keep in mind that selecting team members is not merely about filling roles; it's about forming relationships built on trust and respect. As a leader, you should be open about your expectations while also allowing space for candidates to express their own values and aspirations. This dialogue not only helps identify alignment but also sets the tone for transparency within your future team.

As you refine your selection process, consider implementing feedback mechanisms where current team members can weigh in on new hires. This practice not only enhances buy-in from existing staff but also promotes a sense of ownership among them regarding team dynamics. When everyone feels invested in the decision-making process, it creates an atmosphere of collaboration right from the start.

Finally, remember that selecting team members is an ongoing

process rather than a one-time event. Regularly reassess your team's composition to ensure it continues to align with evolving organizational goals and cultural shifts. Adaptability is key; as circumstances change, so too should your approach to leadership and team building.

Are You Ready to Make Tough Decisions?

Navigating Tough Decisions in Team Formation

Building a successful team is not just about gathering skilled individuals; it's about **making the right choices** that align with your organization's culture and goals. As a young leader, you may feel the pressure to fill roles quickly, often leading to hasty decisions that can have lasting consequences. It's essential to recognize that *every choice you make impacts the dynamic of your team*, so take the time to reflect on what each candidate brings to the table.

When faced with tough decisions in team formation, consider what attributes are necessary for success. Think beyond technical skills and experience. Are they adaptable? Do they communicate well? Can they collaborate effectively? These qualities are often just as crucial as hard skills. In many cases, you'll need to weigh potential over past performance. A candidate with less experience might show a strong willingness to learn and adapt, which could ultimately benefit the team more than hiring someone simply because they have a longer resume.

Trust your instincts, but also back them up with clear criteria. Create a rubric or checklist that outlines the qualities you're looking for in candidates. This structured approach helps minimize bias and allows you to evaluate each candidate fairly against the same standards. Additionally, involving other team members in the selection process can provide valuable perspectives and help foster a sense of ownership among existing staff.

Don't shy away from difficult conversations during this process. If someone seems like a poor fit, it's vital to address it directly rather than glossing over concerns for the sake of politeness. You might find that a straightforward discussion can clarify whether reservations are based on misunderstandings or legitimate concerns about compatibility with your team's culture.

It's also crucial to consider how potential hires will fit within existing dynamics. Each individual brings unique strengths and weaknesses; understanding how these will interact can help prevent conflicts down the line. For example, if you already have strong personalities on your team, adding another dominant voice might create friction instead of fostering collaboration. Balance is key.

Making tough decisions also means acknowledging that sometimes a candidate who appears ideal on paper may not be right for your specific context. The best leaders know when to pivot and adjust their plans based on real-time insights and feedback from their teams. You have the authority to change course if something doesn't feel right—trust that gut feeling.

Lastly, remember that every decision has its trade-offs. No hire will be perfect; there will always be challenges that come with new dynamics. However, approaching these challenges with a proactive mindset will enable you to guide your team through any obstacles that arise post-hire.

By understanding the importance of making tough decisions in team formation, you empower yourself as a leader capable of building cohesive teams aligned with your organization's vision and mission. Embrace this responsibility; it is one of the most significant steps you can take toward effective leadership in your career journey.

Creating a Collaborative Atmosphere

Managing team dynamics is essential for fostering a productive working environment. When you step into a leadership role, it's crucial to recognize that each individual brings their own personality, strengths, and challenges to the table. Your first task is to create an atmosphere where everyone feels valued and empowered. **Encouraging open communication** is a foundational step in achieving this. Make it clear that team members can voice their opinions without fear of judgment. This not only builds trust but also encourages collaboration, leading to more innovative solutions.

Diversity plays a pivotal role in team dynamics. A diverse team can offer a range of perspectives, which is invaluable when tackling complex problems. However, diversity alone isn't enough; it must be managed effectively. Pay attention to the different backgrounds and experiences of your team members. Foster an environment where differences are celebrated rather than ignored. This can be achieved through team-building exercises that highlight individual strengths and promote understanding among members.

Navigating Conflict with Purpose

Conflict is inevitable in any team setting, but how you handle it can make or break your team's productivity. **Addressing conflicts early on** prevents them from escalating into larger issues that could disrupt team cohesion. Encourage your team to approach disagreements constructively by focusing on the problem rather than personal attributes. Teach them to use "I" statements instead of "you" statements; this shifts the conversation from blame to resolution. For example, saying, "I feel overlooked when my ideas aren't considered", fosters dialogue rather than defensiveness.

As a leader, it's important to model effective conflict resolution skills yourself. When you demonstrate how to address disagreements constructively, your team will likely follow suit. Use real-life examples during discussions to illustrate how conflicts were resolved positively in the past. This transparency will encourage your team members to engage in healthy discussions rather than resorting to avoidance or hostility.

Building Trust Through Accountability

Trust within a team is cultivated over time but can be easily damaged if not nurtured properly. One of the most effective ways to build trust is by promoting **accountability** among team members. Set clear expectations regarding roles and responsibilities so everyone knows what's expected of them and each other. When individuals take ownership of their tasks and follow through on commitments, it reinforces reliability within the group.

Encourage peer accountability as well. Create opportunities for team members to hold one another responsible for their contributions while offering support when needed. This collaborative approach not only enhances trust but also strengthens relationships within the team.

Encouraging Continuous Feedback

Feedback should be viewed as an ongoing conversation rather than a formal event reserved for performance reviews. Establish a culture where constructive feedback is regularly shared among team members at all levels. **This practice not only aids personal growth but also improves overall team performance** by allowing issues to be addressed promptly before they escalate.

Use various methods for providing feedback—both formal and informal—to keep communication fluid and adaptable to different situations and personalities within your team. Encourage self-reflection as well; ask your teammates how they think they're performing and what areas they believe need improvement.

Celebrating Successes Together

Recognizing achievements—big or small—can significantly enhance morale and foster a sense of belonging within the team. Take time to celebrate successes together; this could be through simple acknowledgements during meetings or more structured events like recognition ceremonies or outings.

By publicly recognizing contributions, you reinforce positive behavior while motivating others to strive for excellence as well. Celebrations don't always have to be grand gestures; even small tokens of appreciation can go a long way in making individuals feel valued and connected.

Embracing Adaptability

Finally, remember that managing dynamics isn't about sticking rigidly to one approach; it requires adaptability as circumstances change and new challenges arise. Be prepared to shift strategies based on feedback from your team or changes in organizational goals.

Flexibility demonstrates strength. As leaders navigate these dynamics with resilience, they inspire their teams to do the same, creating an environment where everyone feels empowered to tackle challenges head-on while working cohesively towards common objectives.

Incorporating these principles into your leadership style will not only help manage dynamics effectively but will also create an environment where everyone feels included—a necessity for any thriving organization moving forward together toward success.

Navigating the nuances of team formation can be a daunting task, especially for young leaders stepping into their roles with high expectations yet limited experience. Embracing the challenge of selecting the right team members is crucial, not only for the immediate success of the project but for the long-term health of the organization. By focusing on aligning new recruits with the organization's culture and goals, leaders can lay a solid foundation for a dynamic and productive team environment.

The Route to a Unified Team

Step 1: Define Organizational Culture and Core Values

Start by **crystallizing what your organization stands for**—its mission, values, and the workplace atmosphere you want to cultivate. This clarity will serve as your compass in navigating through the sea of potential candidates, helping you identify those who will thrive within your company's unique environment.

Step 2: Outline Required Skills and Experiences

Next, pinpoint the specific skills and experiences essential for the roles you need to fill. This step ensures that your team not only fits culturally but is also equipped to meet your organizational goals effectively. Remember, a well-rounded team is like a well-tuned orchestra; every member plays a critical role in the harmony of the group.

Step 3: Craft a Structured Recruitment Process

Develop a recruitment strategy that includes detailed job descriptions and a consistent interview protocol. This structure will aid in objectively evaluating candidates and will help maintain focus on both the cultural fit and the technical qualifications necessary for the role.

Step 4: Conduct Insightful Interviews

During interviews, assess candidates' responses to situational questions to gauge their problem-solving and interpersonal skills. This approach helps reveal how they might react under pressure or collaborate within team settings, which is invaluable for predicting their potential success in your organization.

Step 5: Debrief and Decide Collectively

After interviews, gather your hiring team to discuss each candidate's merits and fit for your organization. This collaborative evaluation can provide new insights and help in making a well-rounded decision.

Step 6: Communicate Decisions Effectively

Once a decision is made, inform all candidates promptly about the outcome. Providing feedback, especially to those not selected, reflects well on your organization and helps maintain goodwill in the professional community.

Step 7: Onboard with Emphasis on Culture

For those joining your team, ensure their first experience is welcoming and informative. An effective onboarding process that immerses new hires into your organizational culture can significantly influence their ability to integrate smoothly and contribute quickly.

Step 8: Monitor, Evaluate, and Adjust

Finally, keep a close eye on team dynamics and individual performances. Be prepared to make adjustments as necessary to maintain team harmony and productivity. This ongoing evaluation is key to fostering a resilient and adaptive team.

By following these steps, leaders can more effectively navigate the complexities of team formation. Remember, every member you choose is a critical ingredient in the recipe for your team's success. Being thoughtful and systematic in this process not only enhances your leadership capabilities but also sets the stage for achieving remarkable organizational outcomes.

As we continue our journey through "Master Key Leadership Skills Quickly and Confidently with Timeless Lessons from Route 17", remember that leadership is not just about making decisions but making them count. It's about steering your team through ups and downs while keeping everyone aligned with the broader vision. The skills you hone today will define the leader you become tomorrow.

Chapter Five

PROTECT THE PLAY

Can a Leader Protect Their Team Like a Lineman protects the quarterback?

The sun was blazing down on the practice field, and I could feel the heat radiating off the grass as I crouched low in my stance. As an offensive lineman, I didn't have the glamour of scoring touchdowns or the thrill of catching long passes, but I knew my role was just as important. My job was simple: protect the quarterback. And I took pride in it. Every block, every shove, every ounce of strength I had went into making sure my quarterback had the time and space to execute the play.

Fast forward to years later, and I found myself coaching young linemen on the fundamentals of their positions. Watching those kids hunker down, learning to communicate, move in unison, and trust each other reminded me of the lessons football had taught me—lessons that would shape how I approach operations leadership, both for internal teams and external customers.

"Protect the play!" I yelled from the sidelines, my voice cutting through the sound of helmets clashing and feet pounding against the turf. It wasn't just about keeping the quarterback upright; it was about understanding your role, owning it, and doing your job so that the entire team could succeed.

Leadership in operations is no different. Whether you're working internally with your team or supporting external customers, every leader has a responsibility to protect the play. It's not about shielding people from every challenge or making their work easier—it's about creating an environment where they can perform at their best. Just like an offensive lineman guards the quarterback, a leader guards their team and their customers from unnecessary distractions, miscommunication, and decisions that could derail success.

I think back to one of the first operations teams I led. We were managing a large distribution centre, ensuring that inventory moved efficiently to fulfil orders for customers. It was a fast-paced environment where mistakes could quickly pile up if processes weren't followed. I'll never forget the day when one of my team leads pulled me aside and said, "I feel like I'm putting out fires all day instead of focusing on what I need to get done."

That hit me hard. As a leader, I wasn't protecting the play. My team couldn't execute because I hadn't cleared the way for them to succeed. I had to step back and reassess how I was supporting my team and our customers. It was a turning point for me—a realization that leadership in operations isn't just about managing processes; it's about removing obstacles and empowering people.

In football, protecting the play meant studying the defence, anticipating their moves, and adjusting our strategy. In operations, it's no different. A good leader has to anticipate challenges, read the room, and adapt quickly. It's about staying one step ahead so your team doesn't have to scramble.

When I coached young linemen, I drilled them on the basics: footwork, hand placement, and communication. "Know your assignment," I'd tell them. "And trust your teammates to know theirs." Those fundamentals apply to operations as well. You need to be clear on your role as a leader, trust your team to handle their responsibilities, and make sure everyone is aligned.

But here's the thing—sometimes the defence breaks through. Sometimes, no matter how well you plan, things don't go the way you expect. That's when true leadership is tested. Do you panic? Do you point fingers? Or do you step up and take the hit?

I'll never forget a situation where my team faced a critical service failure with a major customer. A shipment had been delayed due to a series of errors in our routing system, and the client was furious. It would have been easy to blame the delays on external factors or even on the technology. But that's not leadership. Leadership is stepping up and saying, "This happened on my watch, and here's what we're going to do to fix it." It's owning the failure and using it as an opportunity to improve.

In football, if the quarterback gets sacked, it's on the line. And as a lineman, you don't make excuses; you analyze what went wrong and make adjustments for the next play. Operations leadership is the same. You don't dwell on the failure—you learn from it and move forward.

As a leader, protecting the play means more than just

shielding your team from external challenges. It also means holding them accountable. One of the hardest things about coaching young linemen was teaching them to own their mistakes. "If you miss your block, the whole play falls apart," I'd tell them. It wasn't about making them feel bad; it was about helping them understand the impact of their actions.

The same is true in operations. Accountability isn't about assigning blame—it's about creating a culture where everyone understands their role and takes responsibility for their part. When you protect the play, you're not just guarding your team from failure; you're setting them up for success.

On the practice field, I used to tell my linemen, "You don't have to be the fastest or the strongest, but you do have to be the smartest." Protecting the quarterback isn't just about brute force; it's about strategy, awareness, and execution. In operations, the same principles apply. It's not about doing everything yourself—it's about working smart, anticipating challenges, and trusting your team.

I think about those kids I coached and the pride I felt watching them protect their quarterback, knowing they were part of something bigger than themselves. That's what leadership in operations is all about. It's about understanding that your role isn't to be the star of the show—it's to make sure the people around you have the space, the support, and the confidence to shine.

Whether on the field or in a distribution centre, we're not just protecting a quarterback or a play—we're protecting a team's ability to succeed. Every action we take as leaders, every decision we make, is an opportunity to contribute to something greater than ourselves. Operations leadership is about clearing the path, managing the flow, and ensuring that both internal teams and external customers have what they need to win.

So ask yourself: Are you protecting the play? Are you anticipating challenges and removing obstacles for your team? Are you holding them accountable while giving them the support they need to succeed? Because at the end of the day, leadership isn't about standing in the spotlight—it's about making sure your team has the chance to cross the goal line.

"Leadership isn't about being the star; it's about clearing the way so your team can score. Just like a lineman protects the quarterback, a leader's greatest role is enabling others to succeed." – Quentin J. Walker

Guarding the Core: Why Accountability Isn't Just a Buzzword

In the realm of leadership, accountability is far from a mere checkbox on a list of traits. It's the backbone that supports every successful strategy and action within an organization. As we delve into the nuances of this critical attribute in our journey toward mastering leadership skills, it becomes clear that understanding and implementing accountability is akin to an offensive lineman protecting his quarterback. This chapter aims to unravel the layers of accountability, ensuring that as emerging leaders, you not only grasp its essence but also learn to wield it effectively within your teams.

The role of accountability in leadership can be distilled into a simple truth: **it builds trust**. When leaders demonstrate accountability, they send a powerful message to their team members—that each person's role is respected and crucial to the collective success. This fosters a culture where individuals feel valued and motivated to reciprocate with their own responsible actions.

The Framework of Accountability

At its core, accountability in leadership involves owning both the decisions made and the outcomes achieved—good or bad. This chapter explores how you can *embrace* this responsibility wholeheartedly. By establishing clear roles and responsibilities, leaders can create an environment where expectations are understood and everyone knows what they need to do. This clarity not only enhances efficiency but also reduces confusion, leading to more effective teamwork.

Another focal point is teaching strategies that help maintain this clarity and ensure that each team member upholds their end of the bargain. We will look into practical ways leaders can keep everyone aligned with the team's goals and accountable for their contributions. This proactive approach prevents issues from escalating and helps maintain momentum towards achieving team objectives.

Handling Failures Like a Pro

No leadership discussion is complete without addressing how to handle setbacks. In this chapter, we develop a framework for dealing with failures constructively. Instead of fostering a culture of blame, effective leaders use setbacks as valuable learning opportunities. By doing so, they not only improve team resilience but also enhance their capability to tackle future challenges more adeptly.

Handling feedback is another crucial aspect covered here. Constructive criticism is a goldmine for growth; however, it requires an open mind and a secure sense of self from both the giver and receiver. We will discuss how leaders can foster an environment where feedback is regularly exchanged in a manner that promotes improvement rather than dissent.

Conclusion: The Accountability Advantage

In essence, this chapter serves as your guide to understanding why accountability is indispensable in leadership and how you can apply it comprehensively within your own teams. By mastering these elements, you will not just be directing people but leading them—a subtle yet profound difference that defines great leaders.

By committing to these principles, you will find yourself better equipped to navigate any challenges that come your way, ensuring that you not only reach your destination but also enjoy the journey there with your team fully intact and functioning at its best.

Accountability is a crucial pillar of effective leadership. It's about taking ownership of your responsibilities and ensuring that your team can rely on you. This concept often feels daunting for new leaders, especially when faced with the challenges of a dynamic work environment. Yet, understanding accountability is vital; it allows leaders to build trust within their teams and foster an atmosphere where everyone feels empowered to contribute.

When you embrace accountability, you signal to your team that they can depend on you. This isn't just about meeting deadlines or achieving targets; it's about being present and engaged in the process. For instance, if a project hits a snag, an accountable leader steps up rather than shifting blame. They assess the situation, learn from it, and communicate transparently with their team. This approach not only resolves issues but also cultivates a culture of collective responsibility.

To implement accountability effectively, start by modeling the behavior you expect from your team. If you're consistent in your commitments and open about your challenges, your team is more likely to mirror that behavior. *Leading by example* creates a ripple effect that encourages others to own their roles within the group. You set the standard for how accountability looks in action.

A significant aspect of fostering accountability is establishing clear expectations from the outset. Make sure each team member understands their responsibilities and how they fit into the larger objectives of the organization. When roles are well-defined, it minimizes confusion and promotes individual ownership. Encourage team members to voice concerns if they feel unclear about their tasks; this openness fosters a proactive approach to accountability.

It's also essential to create an environment where feedback is both given and received constructively. This means creating opportunities for discussions about performance—both positive and negative—without fear of repercussions. When feedback becomes part of the regular dialogue, it reinforces a sense of responsibility and encourages continuous improvement among team members.

Recognizing achievements is just as important as addressing shortcomings. Celebrating successes reinforces accountability by showing that hard work is valued and recognized. Acknowledging individual contributions can motivate others to step up and take ownership of their roles, thus enhancing overall team performance.

Accountability doesn't imply perfection; rather, it acknowledges that mistakes will happen but emphasizes learning from them. A leader who embraces this perspective fosters resilience within their team. They encourage experimentation and calculated risk-taking while providing support when things don't go as planned.

As you continue developing your leadership skills, remember that embracing accountability will not only benefit your growth but also strengthen your team's cohesion and effectiveness. As young leaders navigate the complexities of their roles, they must recognize that accountability is more than just a duty—it's a pathway to building lasting trust and achieving shared goals.

Are you ready to define roles and responsibilities?

Establish Clear Roles and Responsibilities

One of the most effective strategies for leaders is to **clearly define roles and responsibilities** within the team. When each member knows their specific duties, it reduces ambiguity and fosters a sense of ownership. Start by outlining each person's tasks in detail. This not only clarifies expectations but also allows team members to understand how their contributions fit into the larger goals of the organization. A simple chart or document can serve as a reference point, ensuring that everyone stays aligned and accountable.

Foster Open Communication

Encouraging open lines of communication is essential for upholding team responsibilities. Create an environment where team members feel comfortable discussing their challenges, asking questions, or seeking clarification on their roles. Regular check-ins, whether through one-on-one meetings or team huddles, can help identify any obstacles early on. By promoting a culture of transparency, you empower your team to hold each other accountable and seek support when needed.

Implement Performance Metrics

Using performance metrics can be a game changer in ensuring responsibilities are met. Establish clear, measurable objectives that align with individual roles and the team's overall goals. These metrics provide a framework for evaluation and help track progress over time. When team members see how their performance impacts the larger picture, it cultivates motivation and accountability. Make sure to review these metrics regularly to celebrate successes and identify areas for improvement.

Encourage Peer Accountability

Peer accountability can be an incredibly effective tool in maintaining responsibility within a team. Encourage team members to check in with one another about their tasks and progress. This not only builds camaraderie but also creates an environment where everyone feels invested in each other's success. Consider implementing accountability partners or small groups where individuals can discuss their goals and hold each other accountable for meeting them.

Provide Constructive Feedback

Feedback is a vital component of accountability. Establish a routine for providing constructive feedback that focuses on behaviours rather than personal attributes. When giving feedback, aim for specificity—point out what was done well and where improvements can be made. This approach helps individuals understand how to adjust their actions moving forward while reinforcing positive behaviours that align with their responsibilities.

Lead by Example

As a leader, your actions set the tone for the entire team. Model accountability by taking ownership of your responsibilities and being transparent about your own challenges. When team members see you admitting mistakes or seeking help, it creates an atmosphere where they feel safe doing the same. Your commitment to accountability will encourage them to follow suit, ultimately strengthening the entire team's performance.

Recognize Achievements

Celebrating both individual and collective achievements plays a significant role in reinforcing accountability within the team. Acknowledge when someone fulfils their responsibilities exceptionally well or when the group meets its goals together. Public recognition not only boosts morale but also demonstrates that fulfilling one's duties leads to positive outcomes—a powerful motivator for continued effort and commitment.

Adaptability is Key

While clarity in roles is crucial, it's equally important to remain adaptable as circumstances change. Encourage flexibility among your team members so they can adjust to shifting priorities or unexpected challenges without losing sight of their core responsibilities. Being open to change while maintaining accountability ensures that your team remains effective even in dynamic environments.

By implementing these strategies, young leaders can create a culture of accountability that enhances trust within the team and drives overall success. Each step reinforces the importance of individual contributions while fostering an environment where collaboration thrives—ultimately allowing everyone on the team to flourish together.

The Accountability Framework for Leadership

Creating a culture of accountability within a team is essential for effective leadership. This framework consists of four interrelated components: Responsibility, Ownership, Transparency, and Continuous Improvement. Each element plays a critical role in fostering an environment where team members feel empowered to take charge of their contributions while also learning from both successes and setbacks.

Responsibility

Responsibility is the foundation of accountability. It begins with clearly defining roles and expectations within the team. When leaders articulate specific duties and responsibilities, everyone knows what is expected of them. This clarity helps reduce confusion and miscommunication. Team members can focus on their tasks without second-guessing their roles, which enhances productivity.

In practice, this means leaders must take the time to outline individual and collective responsibilities during team meetings or through written communication. When everyone understands their specific contributions toward team goals, it sets a solid groundwork for accountability to flourish.

Ownership

Ownership takes responsibility a step further by encouraging team members to take charge of their actions and outcomes. In an accountable environment, individuals feel a personal stake in the team's success. They are not just completing tasks; they are actively engaging with their work and taking pride in what they produce.

Leaders can foster a sense of ownership by recognizing accomplishments and encouraging initiative. When team members feel that their input matters and that they have the freedom to make decisions within their roles, they become more invested in the outcomes. This heightened engagement leads to improved performance and morale.

Transparency

Transparency is about open communication and sharing information relevant to decision-making processes. Leaders who practice transparency create an atmosphere of trust where team members feel comfortable voicing concerns or asking questions. This openness fosters collaboration and ensures that everyone is aligned toward common objectives.

To implement transparency effectively, leaders should share updates about projects, changes in direction, or organizational challenges. Regular check-ins can facilitate dialogue among team members, helping them understand how their efforts contribute to larger goals. By being transparent about both successes and failures, leaders nurture trust within the team.

Continuous Improvement

Continuous Improvement is the final component of this accountability framework. This concept emphasizes learning from experiences—both positive and negative. Leaders should encourage regular feedback sessions where team members can reflect on what worked well and what didn't, fostering an environment where mistakes are viewed as learning opportunities rather than failures.

Creating systems for feedback involves establishing regular intervals for reviews—be it weekly meetings or quarterly assessments—where constructive discussions can take place. By prioritizing growth through feedback, teams can adapt more effectively to challenges and improve overall performance over time.

The dynamics among these components create a robust framework for accountability in leadership. **Responsibility lays the groundwork**, while **Ownership builds engagement; Transparency fosters trust**, and **Continuous Improvement drives growth**. Together, these elements create a cohesive system that enhances teamwork, motivation, and effectiveness.

As this framework operates over time, it produces positive feedback loops that reinforce accountability across all levels of leadership. For example, when leaders model transparency by openly discussing challenges faced by the organization, it encourages team members to take ownership of their roles even more seriously. This interplay cultivates stability within the group as individuals continuously strive for improvement.

The practical implications of this framework extend beyond mere task completion; they have significant impacts on overall business success. By instilling accountability at every level of leadership, organizations can enhance collaboration among teams while driving performance toward shared goals.

In summary, adopting this Accountability Framework can lead to stronger teams that are motivated to uphold responsibilities while embracing opportunities for growth through feedback mechanisms. As young leaders navigate their paths ahead, understanding how these components interact will empower them to build effective teams capable of achieving remarkable results together.

As we wrap up our discussion on leadership accountability, it's essential to recognize that the core of effective leadership lies in embracing responsibility and fostering a culture where every team member understands and upholds their duties. By instilling accountability, leaders not only protect the integrity of their team's mission but also cultivate an environment ripe for success and mutual trust.

Accountability is not just a buzzword; it's the foundation upon which reliable and resilient teams are built. When leaders step up to own their actions and decisions, they set a powerful example for their team. This creates a ripple effect, encouraging team members to also take responsibility seriously, which in turn enhances overall performance.

Moreover, by **clearly defining roles and responsibilities**, leaders eliminate confusion and align team efforts towards common goals.

This clarity is crucial, especially when navigating challenging projects or tight deadlines. Each team member knows exactly what is expected of them, which simplifies decision-making and accelerates progress.

Handling failures and feedback with grace and constructiveness is another critical aspect of leadership. Instead of viewing setbacks as roadblocks, effective leaders see them as opportunities to learn and grow. This approach not only helps in refining strategies and improving skills but also strengthens the team's resilience in the face of future challenges.

Remember, leadership is not about having all the answers; it's about guiding your team through the highs and lows with confidence and integrity. As you move forward, keep these principles in mind. *Embrace accountability, clarify responsibilities, and approach failures as stepping stones.* By doing so, you will not only achieve your objectives but also inspire those around you to rise to their full potential.

Let this be a reminder that your role as a leader is vital. Your ability to uphold these values will define your journey and the success of your team. Let's strive to be leaders who not only aim for success but also nurture environments where trust, responsibility, and growth flourish.

Chapter Six

FINDING MY WAY

The wind brushed against my face as I stepped out onto the cracked pavement, 10 years old and clutching a small handful of pennies—exactly twenty-five to be precise. That was the cost of a bus ride on Route 17, and counting out those coins had become a ritual. Back then, the world was big, loud, and sometimes overwhelming, but riding the bus gave me a sense of control and purpose. It wasn't just transportation—it was independence.

Route 17 wasn't just a bus ride; it was a lesson. I'd watch the other passengers come and go, some shuffling on with heavy bags, others laughing with friends or quietly lost in thought. It was my first experience seeing the diversity of people, each with their own destination and their own reason for being there. And I realized, even then, that not everyone was going to the same place.

That bus ride was where I first learned how to navigate not just the streets but the people around me. You see when you're six, carrying enough money for one ride and maybe a snack later, you have to make choices. Did I get off early and walk to save a few coins, or did I stay on and risk running out of bus fare for the trip back? Every decision mattered.

Fast forward to today, and I see that same principle in leadership. Whether I'm leading a team through an operational challenge or helping someone develop their skills, it's all about making decisions with limited resources—time, energy, and sometimes patience. And just like that little boy on the bus, I've learned that not everyone can come along for the ride.

When I think back to those early days, one moment stands out. One afternoon, as I clutched my coins and waited for the bus, an older woman with bags of groceries struggled to climb aboard. The driver waited patiently as she fumbled with her change, and other passengers either looked away or offered quiet words of encouragement. In that moment, I saw something profound: not everyone could move at the same pace, and sometimes, you had to adjust to accommodate others.

But here's the flip side—there were also people on that bus who didn't care. They grumbled loudly, complaining about the delay. It was my first real glimpse of the two kinds of people you encounter in life: those who help and those who hinder. That stuck with me.

Years later, I found myself leading my team. I had big dreams for what we could accomplish, but I quickly learned that ambition wasn't enough. Like that bus ride, not everyone was moving at the same pace, and not everyone shared the same destination.

I remember one team member in particular who had incredible technical skills but resisted any kind of collaboration. Every team meeting felt like a tug-of-war—his ideas versus everyone else's. At first, I thought I could fix it. I spent extra time with him, trying to pull him into the fold, but his resistance didn't budge. Eventually, I had to make the tough decision to remove him from the team. It wasn't easy, but the difference it made was immediate. The remaining team members flourished without the tension, and the project moved forward seamlessly.

That's when I realized that leadership isn't just about adding the right people—it's about knowing when to subtract the wrong ones.

Back on Route 17, I'd see passengers who brought a certain energy to the ride. Some were kind, chatting with others or offering their seats to someone in need. Others were disruptive, loud, or confrontational, making the ride feel longer and more difficult than it needed to be. Even as a kid, I could tell the difference, and it taught me something crucial: energy matters.

As a leader, it's your job to protect the energy of your team. You have to pay attention to how people show up, not just in terms of skills but in how they contribute to the overall environment. A team can't thrive if one person's negativity or lack of engagement drags everyone else down.

I see a lot of young leaders struggle with this. They want to please everyone, to bring every voice to the table, even when some of those voices aren't helping. It's a noble instinct, but it's not sustainable. You can't take everyone with you.

I think back to one particular project early in my career. It was a high-stakes launch for a major customer, and the pressure was intense. I had assembled a team I thought was perfect—smart, skilled, and diverse in their perspectives. But as the project went on, cracks began to show. One person was consistently missing deadlines, another was overly critical of everyone else's work, and the dynamic quickly became toxic.

I hesitated to address it at first, afraid of rocking the boat. But the more I waited, the worse it got. Finally, I sat down with each team member one-on-one. For the underperformers, we worked out a plan to improve, and to their credit, they rose to the challenge. For the person creating tension, it became clear that they weren't a fit for the team, and I had to remove them from the team. It was uncomfortable, but it was necessary. The team flourished after that, delivering one of the best projects I've ever been a part of.

As a six-year-old on Route 17, I didn't know the word "leadership," but I understood the concept. I learned to watch, to listen, and to make decisions based on what was best for the journey. Now, as a leader, I carry those lessons with me.

Not everyone can come to the BBQ, and not everyone can ride the bus. Leadership means making the tough calls about who gets a seat and who doesn't. It means recognizing when someone's energy or actions are holding the team back and having the courage to address it.

As I reflect on those early rides, I realize how much they shaped my approach to leadership. It's not just about getting to the destination—it's about choosing the right people to take the journey with you. Because when you surround yourself with the right team, the ride is smoother, the energy is better, and the destination feels that much more rewarding.

"Leadership is about choosing the right passengers for the

journey, knowing when to lift others up, and having the courage to let go of those who weigh the team down. Not everyone can ride the bus—but those who do make all the difference." – Quentin J. Walker

Not Everyone Makes the Guest List

Navigating team dynamics is much like hosting a selective gathering—you aim to invite those who not only enjoy the party but also contribute to its atmosphere. In the realm of leadership, understanding how to assemble and manage a team is not just about grouping people together; it's about curating a collective that harmoniously drives toward shared goals. This chapter delves into the nuanced art of team selection, emphasizing why discernment in leadership can be as crucial as direction.

Strategic Team-Building: A cornerstone of effective leadership, this involves more than just selecting individuals based on their skills or achievements. It requires a deep understanding of each potential team member's compatibility with the group's culture and objectives. A well-composed team can navigate challenges more fluidly, leveraging diverse strengths to overcome obstacles.

Building Resilience Through Unknowns

One of the first lessons in leadership is resilience, which often springs from stepping into unfamiliar territories. Leaders must learn not only to survive but to thrive amid uncertainties. This chapter will explore strategies for fostering resilience preparing leaders to handle situations that lack clear paths or precedents. By embracing these challenges, leaders can sculpt a responsive and adaptable team.

Independence in Decision-Making

A key attribute of any leader is the capacity for independent decision-making. This trait becomes particularly significant when decisions need alignment not just with personal vision but also with that of the organization and its members' welfare. We will discuss how nurturing independence in decision-making can serve as the backbone for strong leadership, providing insights into balancing guidance with autonomy.

The Role of Calculated Risks

Innovation is often born from risks—but not just any risks: calculated ones. Encouraging your team to take informed, strategic risks can lead to breakthroughs and significant advancements. This segment will shed light on methods to assess and manage risks effectively, ensuring they align with long-term objectives while promoting an innovative mindset among team members.

Team Dynamics and Culture Fit: Just as not everyone you know is invited to a personal celebration, not every talented individual may fit well within your existing team framework. The essence of strategic team-building lies in recognizing which potential members will enhance the dynamics and which might hinder them. It's about foreseeing interactions and outcomes, much like a chess player anticipates moving several turns ahead.

The focus here is clear: leadership is less about commanding an army and more about directing a symphony. Each member plays a critical role, and their harmonious interaction under thoughtful direction creates impactful results. Thus, effective leadership involves making tough choices about who will help achieve these results most cohesively.

In wrapping up this introduction, remember that building an

effective team is an ongoing process—a continuous cycle of assessment, adjustment, and evolution. As we move forward in this chapter, keep these foundational ideas at the forefront: resilience through adversity, independence in decision-making, and the judicious embrace of calculated risks are all part of steering your ship through both calm and stormy waters.

Navigating through unknown and challenging situations is a fundamental skill for any leader. **Resilience** is not just about enduring difficulties; it's about learning to adapt and thrive amid uncertainty. This requires a proactive mindset that embraces challenges as opportunities for growth. When faced with unexpected obstacles, it's essential to maintain a level-headed approach, enabling you to assess the situation calmly and devise effective strategies.

One of the first steps in building resilience is understanding that setbacks are part of the journey. Instead of viewing them as failures, consider them as valuable lessons. Each obstacle presents a chance to refine your skills and develop new strategies for overcoming similar challenges in the future. This shift in perspective can transform your approach to leadership. Rather than fearing the unknown, you begin to see it as a landscape ripe for exploration.

The process of navigating uncertainty often involves stepping outside your comfort zone. Embracing discomfort can feel unsettling, but it is here that real growth occurs. Imagine leading a team through a complex project with tight deadlines or untested technologies. The pressure might be intense, but these moments can foster resilience within yourself and your team. Encourage open communication, solicit feedback, and create an environment where team members feel safe sharing their concerns and ideas.

Building resilience also hinges on self-awareness. Recognizing your strengths and weaknesses allows you to manage stress effectively. When faced with challenges, assess how you typically respond under pressure. Are you inclined to withdraw or become defensive? Understanding these tendencies enables you to adjust your reactions and cultivate a more constructive response when faced with difficulties.

Another key element is developing a support network. Surrounding yourself with individuals who inspire and challenge you can provide both perspective and encouragement during tough times. Leaning on mentors or peers who have navigated similar situations can offer insights that help you steer through uncertainties more effectively. Remember, leadership doesn't mean going it alone; it's about fostering connections that enhance your resilience.

Establishing **clear goals** is also crucial when facing uncertainty. Having defined objectives provides direction amid chaos. These goals serve as anchors that keep you focused on what matters most, even when distractions abound. By breaking larger tasks into manageable steps, you can maintain momentum despite the challenges that arise along the way.

Finally, cultivate an attitude of gratitude and positivity within your team. Acknowledging small victories fosters a culture where resilience flourishes. Celebrate progress and encourage each other during tough times; this camaraderie strengthens bonds and bolsters collective resolve in facing adversity together.

Are You Ready to Embrace Independence?

Embracing Independence in Leadership

In the realm of leadership, **independence and self-reliance in decision-making** are not just desirable traits; they are essential. When you take on a leadership role, you often face complex situations where the right path isn't always clear. In these moments, relying solely on others for guidance can lead to confusion or stagnation. Instead, developing your ability to make informed decisions independently will empower you and inspire confidence in those you lead.

One of the first steps towards independence is cultivating a sense of ownership over your choices. Each decision you make reflects your values and vision. Embrace this responsibility. Rather than deferring to popular opinion or seeking validation from others, trust your instincts and the knowledge you've gained through experience. This doesn't mean ignoring feedback; rather, it means filtering that feedback through your own understanding and goals.

Self-reliance doesn't imply isolation. It's important to recognize that collaboration has its place in decision-making. However, there will be times when you must stand firm in your convictions, especially when facing challenges that require swift action. By balancing input from your team with your independent judgment, you can create a dynamic where ideas flow freely while still maintaining the clarity of vision needed to move forward decisively.

Facing uncertainty is a part of leadership that can be daunting. Often, leaders feel pressure to project certainty even when they themselves are unsure. **Acknowledging this uncertainty is crucial**. It allows you to approach problems with a clear mind and assess options without being paralyzed by fear of failure. Embracing independence means being comfortable with making decisions despite not having all the answers upfront.

The benefits of self-reliance extend beyond personal development; they also foster trust within your team. When team members see you making confident decisions based on sound reasoning, they are more likely to respect your leadership and follow your direction. This creates a culture of accountability where everyone feels empowered to contribute their perspectives while understanding that, ultimately, decisions rest with the leader.

To strengthen your independence in decision-making, consider adopting a structured approach when faced with choices. Start by clearly defining the problem at hand and gathering relevant information before evaluating potential solutions. This method not only aids clarity but also reinforces confidence in your conclusions. As you practice this process consistently, it will become second nature.

Mistakes are part of growth, so don't shy away from them. Each misstep provides valuable lessons that will enhance your decision-making skills over time. Rather than viewing mistakes as failures, see them as opportunities for reflection and learning—a vital part of becoming a more adept leader.

As you cultivate independence and self-reliance in decision-making, remember that *this journey is ongoing*. Regularly seek ways to challenge yourself while also being mindful of how much input from others you're willing to incorporate into your process. The balance between collaboration and independent thought is nuanced but crucial for effective leadership.

In sum, embracing independence doesn't mean shutting out diverse perspectives; it means confidently integrating them into your decision-making framework while staying true to your vision and values. This approach will serve you well as a leader navigating complex environments—enabling not only personal growth but also empowering those around you to thrive alongside you on this path forward.

Embracing Calculated Risks

In leadership, taking risks is an essential part of fostering growth and innovation. However, it's important to distinguish between reckless decisions and calculated risks. *Calculated risks* involve thoughtful consideration and strategic planning, allowing leaders to venture into the unknown while minimizing potential downsides. By understanding the landscape and potential outcomes, leaders can make informed choices that not only benefit their teams but also encourage a culture of creativity and experimentation.

A crucial aspect of encouraging calculated risks is creating an environment where team members feel safe to express their ideas. When individuals know that their contributions will be valued, they are more likely to step outside their comfort zones. This sense of psychological safety fosters open communication, which is vital for innovative thinking. Leaders should actively promote discussions around new ideas and solutions, ensuring that every voice is heard and considered.

Moreover, it's essential to set clear parameters around risk-taking. Establishing guidelines helps team members understand what kinds of risks are acceptable and what resources are available for experimentation. For instance, if a team is exploring a new marketing strategy, defining the budget limits and timeframes can prevent chaos while still allowing room for innovation. By providing structure, leaders empower their teams to explore new avenues without fear of overstepping boundaries.

Learning from failures is another critical component of taking calculated risks. When a risk doesn't pay off, it's easy to view it as a setback. However, leaders should frame these moments as opportunities for learning and growth. Encouraging teams to analyze what went wrong can lead to valuable insights that inform future decisions. This approach not only builds resilience but also strengthens the team's problem-solving capabilities.

In addition to individual growth, calculated risk-taking can significantly enhance team dynamics. When team members see each other taking bold steps and navigating challenges together, it fosters camaraderie and trust. Celebrating successes—no matter how small—

reinforces this behaviour and motivates others to take similar leaps in the future. Recognizing effort in the face of uncertainty cultivates an atmosphere where innovation thrives.

As a leader, it's also beneficial to model calculated risk-taking yourself. Sharing your experiences with both successes and failures demonstrates vulnerability and authenticity. This transparency encourages your team members to take their own chances while knowing they have your support regardless of the outcome. Leadership isn't just about making decisions; it's about showing others how to navigate uncertainty with confidence.

Ultimately, encouraging calculated risks is about balancing caution with courage. It involves understanding when to push boundaries while maintaining awareness of potential pitfalls. Leaders who master this balance not only drive innovation but also cultivate a resilient culture where creativity flourishes amid challenges. By empowering teams to take informed risks, you position them—and yourself—for long-term success in an ever-evolving landscape.

As you reflect on your own leadership journey, consider how you can integrate calculated risk-taking into your team's routine activities. What structures can you implement? How can you create an environment where ideas flow freely? By prioritizing these elements, you'll not only enhance your leadership effectiveness but also inspire those around you to reach new heights in their pursuits.

As we wrap up this exploration, let's reflect on the powerful lessons we've uncovered together. Building resilience, embracing independence, and encouraging risk-taking are not just strategies; they are essential components in the toolkit of any successful leader. Each of these elements plays a crucial role in shaping a leader who can effectively navigate the complexities of modern leadership landscapes.

Building resilience through challenging situations prepares you to handle unexpected turns and obstacles with grace. Think of it as the shock absorbers in a vehicle, allowing you to ride smoothly over bumps without losing your course. This skill is invaluable when leading a team through periods of uncertainty or change.

Embracing **independence in decision-making** doesn't mean going it alone; rather, it's about trusting your instincts and making informed choices. It's similar to driving on an unfamiliar road but confidently using the tools and knowledge at your disposal to make the journey successful. This independence fosters a sense of reliability and trustworthiness among your team members, who look to you for guidance and vision.

Lastly, the encouragement of **calculated risks** is the spark that ignites innovation and growth. Just as a driver might take a less travelled path to discover a more scenic or quicker route, a leader must sometimes venture beyond the conventional to achieve extraordinary results. This approach not only leads to personal and organizational growth but also inspires your team to think creatively and push boundaries.

As leaders, understanding the dynamics of our team is as crucial as knowing our individual capabilities. Not everyone will fit perfectly into every team scenario, much like not every guest is suitable for every gathering. Strategic team-building, highlighted in the next chapter, involves recognizing and aligning strengths to foster a cohesive and productive environment.

By mastering these skills, you set a strong foundation for yourself and your team, equipped to face whatever the road ahead presents. Each challenge becomes a chance to demonstrate resilience; every decision is an opportunity to display independence; each risk is a potential for substantial growth.

Let these insights guide you as you continue on your journey, knowing that the skills you've honed here are not just theories but practical tools that will serve you well on the path to becoming an impactful leader. Remember, the road to success is often uncharted, but with the right skills and mindset, you can navigate any challenge that comes your way.

Chapter Seven

RIDE THE BUS, KNOW THE ROUTE

When Words Build Walls or Bridges

The winter air bit at my face as I stood at the bus stop, clutching the strap of my bag and glancing down the street for the familiar outline of the Route 17 bus. As a child, I didn't have much to say about leadership or communication. But looking back, those rides taught me lessons I'd lean on for the rest of my life.

Each ride wasn't just about getting from point A to point B—it was about learning to navigate the route. I watched how the drivers communicated with passengers, some with a smile and a joke, others with a curt word that closed off any interaction. I saw how those small exchanges could set the tone for the entire ride.

Fast-forward to today, and I see the parallels in leadership. Knowing the route—understanding the people, the process, and the purpose—is only half the battle. The real challenge lies in how you communicate along the way. Are your words building bridges or creating walls?

I remember one particular day when communication—or the lack of it—nearly derailed my team. It was midwinter, and tensions were already running high. We were deep into an operational overhaul, and every decision felt like a domino that could either set us up for success or knock everything down.

During a morning meeting, a simple misunderstanding turned into a full-blown argument. It started with one team member feeling like their concerns weren't being heard, and before I knew it, voices were raised, and lines were drawn. By the time the meeting ended, the room was heavy with unspoken resentment.

I sat in my office afterwards, replaying the meeting in my mind. The frustration in their voices, the defensiveness in their words—I had seen it all before. I knew that if we didn't address it, the division would only grow.

I thought back to Route 17. As a kid, I'd seen how the bus drivers managed conflicts—sometimes with patience, other times with a sharpness that only made things worse. I learned early that words could either calm the ride or make it bumpier.

The next morning, I called the team together. I stood in front of them, took a deep breath, and said, "Yesterday, we hit a bump in the road. But it's on me to make sure we're back on track." I acknowledged the misunderstanding and explained how we had gotten off course. Then I asked for their input, not just on the process but on how we could communicate better moving forward.

To my surprise, the floodgates opened. One by one, they shared their frustrations—not just about the process but about how we had been working as a team. They weren't just upset about yesterday's meeting; they were carrying weeks, even months, of unresolved tension.

It wasn't easy to hear, but it was necessary. By the end of the meeting, the mood had shifted. It wasn't perfect, but the ice had begun to thaw. The walls that had gone up were starting to come down, brick by brick.

Riding Route 17 taught me that clear communication isn't just about what you say—it's about how you listen. As a kid, I'd watch passengers ask for directions or clarification, and the best drivers took the time to listen and respond thoughtfully. The worst ones barked out answers that left people more confused than before.

Leadership works the same way. People aren't just looking for instructions; they're looking for connection. They want to know that their concerns are heard and that their input matters.

That was a turning point for me. I realized that leadership isn't just about setting the destination—it's about making sure everyone knows the route and feels equipped to navigate it.

One of the most important lessons I've learned is that communication doesn't end once the message is delivered. Just like a bus driver checks their mirrors and listens for feedback, a leader has to pay attention to how their words are received. Are people nodding along but staying silent? Are they asking questions or pushing back?

Those reactions tell you whether the message has landed or if it needs to be clarified. Leadership isn't about saying something once and assuming it sticks—it's about following up, checking in, and adjusting as needed.

Back on Route 17, I'd often watch the driver navigate unexpected detours—construction zones, traffic jams, or passengers with special requests. The best drivers didn't panic; they adjusted, communicated the change, and kept moving forward. That's what leadership is all about. It's not just about sticking to the plan; it's about knowing when to pivot and how to bring everyone along with you.

As a leader, I realized that the key wasn't just knowing the route—it was making sure my team knew it, too. It was about creating an environment where questions were welcome, feedback was valued, and misunderstandings were addressed head-on.

Every bus ride has its bumps, and every team has its conflicts. The question is, how will you handle them? Will your words build walls or bridges?

Looking back, I see how those early lessons on Route 17 shaped my approach to leadership. They taught me that clear and honest communication isn't just a tool—it's the foundation of trust and collaboration.

So, as you lead your own teams, remember this: it's not just about getting to the destination—it's about making sure everyone is on board and knows the route. When everyone is aligned, the ride is smoother, the journey is more enjoyable, and the destination is sweeter.

"Leadership isn't just about knowing the destination—it's about using your words to pave the way. Clear communication builds the bridges that carry your team through every detour and challenge." – Quentin J. Walker

> How can clear communication not only prevent but also repair misunderstandings in times of conflict?

The Unseen Engine of Success: Why Straight Talk Matters in Leadership

In the complex dance of leadership, where every step and turn can lead to myriad outcomes, the clarity of your communication acts as your compass. Effective leaders know that it's not just about giving directions but about ensuring those directions are understood and actionable. **This chapter explores the imperative of clear communication**—a critical component often overlooked yet vital for steering any organization towards its objectives.

The Bedrock of Trust

At the heart of effective leadership lies the ability to foster trust. Trust is not merely about reliability or integrity; it's also about predictability and transparency in interactions. When a leader communicates with clarity and honesty, it sets a foundation where expectations are understood, roles are clear, and objectives are transparent. This environment not only cultivates trust but also empowers team members to perform with confidence and commitment.

Aligning Visions to Actions

Imagine a scenario where everyone in your team knows exactly what they need to do, why they need to do it, and how their actions contribute to the larger goal. This isn't just an ideal; it's a practical outcome of mastering strategic communication. By aligning your words with organizational goals, you ensure that your team's efforts are not just concerted but also coherent with the company's trajectory.

Operational Excellence Through Clarity

Operational intricacies can often become a thorn in a team's side, slowing down processes and causing frustration. Here, the power of straightforward communication becomes evident. When leaders articulate procedures clearly and address issues openly, it leads to faster resolutions and smoother operations. This chapter will delve into how understanding and communicating these intricacies can significantly enhance efficiency.

Every leader embarks on their journey, hoping to steer their team or organization toward success. However, without mastering the art of communication—ensuring that every message is clear as daylight—navigating this path can be more challenging than necessary. By adopting a 'Say It Straight' approach, leaders can avoid the common pitfalls that arise from miscommunications and misinterpretations.

The principles laid out in this chapter are not just theoretical; they are actionable insights backed by real-world applications and results. They serve as your toolkit for not just surviving in the leadership role but thriving through effective communication strategies.

As we progress, remember that **communication is more than just speaking or writing**; it's about ensuring your message lands as intended and fosters an environment conducive to growth and understanding. Let's explore how you can harness this skill to not only meet but exceed your leadership goals.

Mastering awareness of your business environment and organizational goals is essential for effective leadership. Every leader must have a clear understanding of their surroundings—the market trends, customer needs, and competitive landscape. This awareness goes beyond mere observation; it requires active engagement and a willingness to listen to both internal and external stakeholders. When leaders prioritize this understanding, they empower their teams to align their efforts with the organization's vision and objectives.

One of the first steps in developing this awareness is conducting thorough research. Explore industry reports, engage with customers, and analyze competitors' strategies. This research equips leaders with valuable insights that can shape decision-making processes. Additionally, staying updated on current events within the industry helps leaders anticipate changes and adapt proactively. For instance, if a new technology emerges that could disrupt your market, being aware of it early allows you to strategize accordingly.

Furthermore, communication plays a pivotal role in ensuring that everyone within the organization is aligned with its goals. Regularly sharing information about market trends and organizational objectives fosters a culture of transparency. When team members understand the bigger picture, they can make more informed decisions in their respective roles. This not only enhances trust but also strengthens collaboration as individuals work toward common goals.

Leaders should also embrace feedback mechanisms to gauge how well their teams comprehend organizational objectives. Implementing regular check-ins or surveys can provide insights into team members' understanding of company goals. By creating an environment where feedback is valued, leaders can identify gaps in knowledge and address them promptly. This approach not only improves individual performance but also reinforces the collective mission of the organization.

Awareness extends beyond just understanding goals; it encompasses recognizing the diverse perspectives within your team. Each member brings unique experiences and viewpoints that can contribute to a more comprehensive understanding of the business environment. Actively seeking input from team members fosters inclusivity and encourages innovative solutions. Leaders who appreciate these diverse perspectives are better equipped to navigate challenges effectively.

Additionally, aligning personal values with organizational goals creates a strong foundation for commitment among team members. When individuals see how their contributions support overarching objectives, they are more likely to feel invested in their work. Leaders should communicate how each role fits into the larger picture, making it clear that every effort counts towards achieving success.

Moreover, understanding the nuances of your business environment means being aware of potential risks as well as opportunities. Conducting SWOT analyses—assessing strengths, weaknesses, opportunities, and threats—can be instrumental in identifying areas for improvement or growth. A proactive approach to risk management not only protects the organization but also positions it strategically for future endeavours.

Ultimately, mastering awareness involves continuous learning and adaptation. The business landscape is ever-evolving; leaders must remain agile and responsive to changes both within their organizations and in the external environment. By fostering a mindset geared towards growth and openness, leaders can steer their teams toward achieving shared objectives.

Ready to Align Your Team's Efforts?

Aligning Team Efforts with Company Objectives

Successful leadership requires a clear understanding of how team efforts contribute to broader company goals. When leaders take the time to connect their team's daily activities to the overall mission, it fosters a sense of purpose and direction. This alignment not only enhances motivation but also ensures that everyone is pulling in the same direction. It's essential for leaders to articulate how individual tasks fit into the larger picture, bridging the gap between personal contributions and organizational success.

Establishing clear objectives is the first step in this alignment process. Leaders should begin by clearly defining both short-term and long-term goals for their teams. These goals should be specific, measurable, achievable, relevant, and time-bound (SMART). By setting these parameters, leaders provide a roadmap that guides decision-making and prioritization. When team members understand what they are working towards, they can focus their efforts more effectively.

It's important to **communicate these objectives regularly**. Simply sharing goals once at the beginning of a project or during an annual meeting isn't enough. Regular updates and discussions keep everyone informed about progress and any changes in direction. Team meetings can serve as a platform for reinforcing these objectives, allowing space for feedback and questions. This ongoing communication nurtures transparency and trust within the team.

Another critical aspect is ensuring that each team member understands their role in achieving these objectives. Leaders should take the time to discuss individual responsibilities in detail. *How does each person's work contribute to the team's success?* This connection helps individuals see their value within the team structure, boosting morale and encouraging ownership of their tasks.

Engagement is key when aligning efforts with company objectives. Involve your team in discussions about goals—ask for their input and insights on how best to achieve them. This not only creates buy-in but also fosters a collaborative environment where everyone feels valued and heard. When team members are part of the planning process, they are more likely to be committed to executing those plans.

Monitoring progress is equally vital. Leaders should establish metrics that allow them to track how well team efforts align with company objectives over time. Regularly reviewing these metrics creates opportunities for course correction if necessary. If a particular strategy isn't yielding results, it's crucial to reassess and adjust rather than sticking rigidly to a plan that isn't working.

Encouraging adaptability within your team can also enhance alignment with company goals. The business landscape is ever-changing; flexibility allows teams to pivot when unexpected challenges arise or when new opportunities present themselves. Leaders should cultivate an environment where adaptability is seen as a strength rather than a weakness.

Finally, celebrating achievements reinforces alignment with company objectives. Recognizing both small victories and major milestones encourages continued focus on collective goals while enhancing team morale. A simple acknowledgement can remind everyone why their hard work contributes to the organization's success.

In summary, strategically planning and aligning team efforts with overarching company objectives isn't just a one-time task; it's an ongoing process that involves clear communication, engagement, regular monitoring, adaptability, and recognition of achievements. By focusing on these areas, leaders can ensure that their teams remain motivated and aligned with the organization's vision while fostering an atmosphere of trust and collaboration essential for sustained success.

Understanding Operational Intricacies

To lead effectively, it's essential to develop a deep understanding of the operational intricacies within your organization. This knowledge allows you to pinpoint inefficiencies and create solutions that enhance productivity. Recognizing how different departments interact and what processes are in place can unveil opportunities for improvement. When leaders grasp the nuances of their operations, they are better equipped to make informed decisions that positively impact team dynamics and overall performance.

Clear processes are the backbone of efficiency. Without well-defined procedures, confusion can arise, leading to wasted time and resources. Take the time to map out workflows, identify bottlenecks, and establish best practices. By doing so, you not only streamline operations but also create an environment where team members feel empowered and capable of executing their tasks effectively. When everyone understands their role within a clear framework, trust builds naturally.

Furthermore, it's vital to foster open lines of communication regarding operational matters. Encourage team members to share feedback about processes they encounter daily. Their firsthand experience can provide invaluable insights into what works and what doesn't. When leaders actively listen and respond to these concerns, it cultivates a culture of collaboration and continuous improvement. This is where innovation often sparks—by understanding the real challenges faced on the ground.

Embracing technology can significantly enhance operational efficiency. In today's fast-paced business environment, leveraging digital tools can automate repetitive tasks, track performance metrics, and facilitate better communication across teams. Identifying which technologies align with your organizational goals can streamline processes further while freeing up time for strategic thinking. Always assess the tools available and adapt them to fit your team's specific needs.

Another key aspect is aligning operational strategies with organizational objectives. Every process should reflect the company's goals and values. When leaders ensure that day-to-day operations are in harmony with the broader vision, it strengthens cohesion within the team and drives performance towards common outcomes. This alignment acts as a guiding compass for decision-making at all levels.

Training and development play a crucial role in optimizing operations as well. Investing in your team's skills not only enhances their capability but also boosts morale. When employees feel competent in their roles due to adequate training, they're more likely to take ownership of their work and contribute positively to operational success. Providing ongoing learning opportunities keeps everyone engaged and adaptable in a constantly evolving landscape.

Lastly, regularly reviewing operational outcomes is essential for sustained success. Set measurable objectives for your team and assess progress against these benchmarks periodically. This practice not only highlights areas for improvement but also celebrates achievements along the way. Recognizing successes reinforces positive behaviours within the team and motivates individuals to strive for excellence continually.

By developing an understanding of operational intricacies, leaders can streamline processes effectively while enhancing efficiency across their teams. This foundational knowledge enables informed decision-making that aligns with both immediate needs and long-term goals, ultimately fostering a productive work environment where trust thrives and teams excel together.

In mastering the art of leadership, recognizing the significance of our business environment, aligning our team's efforts with broader organizational objectives, and grasping the nuances of operations are pivotal. These aren't just items on a checklist; they are essential skills that breathe life into a leader's vision and strategy.

Awareness of your business environment acts as the compass that guides every decision you make. It's about seeing the bigger picture and understanding how external factors influence your journey. Like a seasoned captain at the helm, a leader must navigate through calm and stormy waters with an unwavering sense of where they are and where they need to go.

Strategic alignment of team efforts ensures that every member not only understands the destination but also their role in getting there. Think of it as a finely tuned orchestra where each musician plays a part in creating a harmonious masterpiece. The synergy that arises from this alignment can propel a company to achieve remarkable feats, turning ambitious goals into tangible successes.

Understanding operational intricacies is akin to knowing every gear and lever in a sophisticated machine. It's about diving deep, beyond surface-level processes, to streamline and refine. This doesn't just enhance efficiency; it fosters a culture of continuous improvement and innovation.

At the core of all these aspects lies effective communication—clear, honest, and purposeful. It's the glue that holds everything together. When communication falters, so does trust and the collective drive towards common goals. Therefore, embracing the 'Say It Straight' principle is not just beneficial; it's indispensable. By ensuring clarity and openness in every interaction, leaders can avoid misunderstandings and build a resilient foundation of trust.

Let's remember that leadership is not about the power one holds but about the empowerment one spreads. As you steer your team through the complexities of the corporate landscape, keep these principles in mind. They are not just strategies; they are the very essence of dynamic and successful leadership.

Now, as we move forward, let these insights not merely linger in your mind but actively shape your leadership style. Equip yourself with these tools, engage deeply with your teams, and watch as you transform challenges into opportunities for growth and success together.

Chapter Eight

YOU VS. YOU

Can Self-Awareness Be the Key to Unlocking True Leadership?

Growing up as an only child, I learned early that responsibility wasn't optional. My mother, a hardworking single parent, poured herself into her job to provide for us. She wasn't just busy—she was relentless. Watching her hustle taught me the value of hard work, but it also meant that a lot of the day-to-day responsibilities fell on me.

At a young age, I learned to make decisions that most kids didn't have to think about. Grocery shopping wasn't just an errand—it was a process. I had to assess what we needed, compare prices, and make the money stretch. Dinner wasn't a meal that magically appeared—it was something I had to plan and execute. Homework? That was on me to manage, along with chores and keeping things in order around the house.

Those experiences weren't just about responsibility; they were about learning to navigate processes and make choices within constraints. And more than that, they were about self-awareness—understanding my role, my decisions, and their impact on the bigger picture.

When you're an operator, processes define your day. From managing workflows to ensuring goals are met, everything depends on clarity and precision. The same was true when I was a kid. I didn't have someone standing over my shoulder, checking my work. It was on me to hold myself accountable, to figure out what needed to be done, and to do it well.

As I grew older, those lessons carried over into my leadership. Early in my career, I assumed leadership was about driving results and holding others accountable. However, I quickly learned that leadership starts with self-awareness. If you can't understand your own actions, habits, and blind spots, you can't effectively lead a process—or a team.

One of the first times I truly understood the importance of self-awareness was during a critical operational challenge. Our team was responsible for revamping a key distribution process that had been causing delays for months. Deadlines were tight, and tensions were high.

I was so focused on hitting the target that I didn't realize how my approach was impacting the team. My urgency came across as impatience, and my constant checking on progress felt like micromanagement. I thought I was keeping everyone on track, but in reality, I was creating friction.

One day, one of my team leads pulled me aside. "You're so focused on the numbers," he said, "that you're missing the bigger picture. The team feels like they're being pushed without support."

It stung to hear, but he was right. I had been so fixated on the process that I wasn't paying attention to the people behind it. That conversation forced me to step back and take a hard look at myself.

Growing up, I didn't have the luxury of ignoring my own actions. If I didn't do the grocery shopping right, we'd run out of food before the next paycheck. If I didn't do my homework, I'd face the consequences at school. As a kid, those moments were about survival, but they were also about learning accountability and self-awareness.

As a leader, I've learned that the same principles apply. Processes succeed or fail based on the choices we make and how we lead through them. And leading effectively starts with understanding how we show up—our tone, our actions, and how they impact the people around us.

I think about another time when self-awareness helped me turn around a struggling process. Our team was responsible for improving inventory management, a critical function for meeting customer demands. The problem was we had conflicting priorities across departments, and communication had broken down.

Instead of tackling the process head-on, I started by reflecting on my own approach. Was I setting clear expectations? Was I fostering collaboration, or was I unintentionally creating silos?

I began holding regular check-ins, not just to monitor progress but to listen to feedback. I asked team members what was working, what wasn't, and how I could better support them. By making adjustments based on their input, we not only fixed the process but also built a stronger team dynamic.

Self-awareness also means being honest about your limitations. Growing up, I knew there were things I wasn't good at—like cooking a perfect dinner—but I still had to try. The same is true in operations. No leader has all the answers, and pretending otherwise only creates more problems.

One of the most valuable lessons I've learned is the power of saying, "I don't know, but I'll find out." It's not a sign of weakness; it's a sign of confidence. A self-aware leader understands their strengths and seeks input where they fall short.

Managing processes requires more than technical expertise—it requires emotional intelligence. I've seen operations leaders who could map out the most efficient workflows but failed to connect with their teams. They treated people like cogs in a machine, and as a result, the machine broke down.

Growing up, I learned that people matter just as much as the process. I saw it in the way my mother worked tirelessly to ensure our needs were met, and in the way, she still found time to listen to me, even after a long day. As a leader, that lesson reminds me that no matter how urgent the task is, taking the time to connect with people is never a waste.

Self-awareness also means managing your emotions. In operations, there are always fires to put out, and it's easy to let frustration get the better of you. Early in my career, I struggled with this. If a process failed, I'd react immediately, sometimes snapping at people who were just as frustrated as I was.

Over time, I realized that leadership requires composure. When things go wrong, your team looks to you for stability. Self-awareness helps you recognize your triggers and respond thoughtfully instead of reacting impulsively.

For me, that often means taking a deep breath, stepping back, and asking myself, "What's the best way to move forward?" It's a simple practice, but it's made a world of difference in how I lead.

Growing up as an only child taught me that responsibility and self-awareness go hand in hand. If I didn't take ownership of my actions, no one else would. That mindset has carried over into my leadership, shaping how I approach processes, teams, and challenges.

As a leader, you'll face countless "you vs. you" moments. Times when you have to confront your habits, question your assumptions, and make choices that challenge your comfort zone. Those moments aren't easy, but they're necessary for growth.

Self-awareness is the foundation of effective leadership. It's what allows you to understand your impact, build trust, and lead with intention. Because at the end of the day, the most important process you'll ever manage is the one within yourself.

"True leadership doesn't begin with issuing commands; it begins with a deep understanding of oneself. Only when you recognize your strengths, weaknesses, and impact can you lead others with purpose and authenticity." – Quentin J. Walker

Could it be that true leadership begins not with asserting

one's vision but understanding oneself fully?

Unlock the Leader Within: Are You Your Greatest Ally or Biggest Obstacle?

As leaders steer their way through the challenging terrain of professional growth, self-awareness emerges not merely as a skill but as a fundamental necessity. It's the engine under your hood powering you through the journey of leadership. This chapter delves into the core of **self-awareness**, emphasizing its vital role in recognizing both your strengths and weaknesses. Understanding these aspects is pivotal not only for personal development but also for sculpting effective leadership.

The Mirror of Leadership: Reflecting on Strengths and Weaknesses

Before you can lead others effectively, you must first lead yourself. This starts with a candid assessment of who you are as a leader. What are your strengths? Where do you falter? These questions aren't just rhetorical—they demand introspection and honesty. By enhancing self-awareness, you equip yourself with the knowledge to leverage your strengths and address your weaknesses head-on.

Strategies for Self-Improvement: Continuous Growth on Your Terms

Leadership is not a static quality but a dynamic skill set that requires continual refinement and adaptation. Implementing strategies for **self-improvement** signifies a commitment to never settling for 'good enough.' It's about setting higher standards for oneself and persistently striving to exceed them. This continuous personal growth ensures that as the challenges evolve, so do you.

Navigating Internal Conflicts: Steering Through Psychological Barriers

Understanding and managing internal conflicts is crucial in maintaining focus and motivation. It's about recognizing the internal dialogues that can either propel you forward or hold you back. Managing these effectively means maintaining control over your psychological landscape, ensuring it drives you towards your goals rather than away from them.

Leadership, at its core, is about understanding yourself to better understand how to lead others. This chapter guides you through the process of self-discovery, offering tools to enhance self-awareness, embrace continuous improvement, and effectively manage internal conflicts. Through this introspective journey, you prepare yourself not just to face external challenges but to conquer the internal ones as well.

By engaging deeply with these themes, leaders can transform their approach from being reactive to proactive, shaping their path with deliberate actions and informed decisions. Remember, every leader's journey is unique; what matters most is how well you know your vehicle—yourself—and how effectively you navigate it towards your desired destination.

In exploring these facets of leadership, this chapter serves as both a mirror and a map: reflecting who you are today and charting a course for who you aspire to become tomorrow. Embrace this journey with openness and curiosity, for it is in understanding the 'You vs. You' dynamic that true leadership flourishes.

Self-awareness is the cornerstone of effective leadership. It involves understanding your own emotions, strengths, weaknesses, and values and how they influence your behaviour and decision-making. Recognizing these aspects allows you to connect more authentically with others and navigate complex situations with confidence. Leaders who lack self-awareness may struggle to build trust or communicate effectively, leading to a disconnect with their teams. Thus, enhancing self-awareness isn't just beneficial; it's essential for anyone aspiring to lead.

To identify your strengths and weaknesses as a leader, start by engaging in honest self-reflection. Consider keeping a journal where you document your daily experiences and feelings. Write about situations that challenged you, how you reacted, and what you learned from those moments. This practice can help highlight patterns in your behaviour and decision-making processes. Over time, you'll notice which qualities serve you well and which areas may need improvement.

Seeking feedback from peers and team members is another powerful way to enhance self-awareness. Constructive criticism can provide insights that you might overlook when evaluating yourself. Create an environment where open dialogue is encouraged, allowing others to share their perspectives without fear of repercussions. By actively listening to their observations about your leadership style, you can gain valuable information about how your actions are perceived.

Understanding the impact of emotional intelligence on leadership is crucial as well. Emotional intelligence encompasses self-regulation, empathy, motivation, social skills, and self-awareness itself. Leaders with high emotional intelligence can manage their emotions effectively and navigate interpersonal relationships judiciously. They are more likely to inspire loyalty in their teams because they understand not just their own feelings but also those of others.

Consider conducting a SWOT analysis (Strengths, Weaknesses, Opportunities, Threats) on yourself as a leader. This structured approach allows you to systematically assess where you excel and where you can improve. You might discover opportunities for growth that align with your strengths while identifying potential threats that could hinder your progress if left unaddressed.

It's also important to remember that self-awareness is not a one-time achievement but a continuous process. As circumstances change—be it through new roles or shifting team dynamics—your strengths and weaknesses may evolve, too. Make it a habit to periodically revisit your self-assessment and seek out new feedback regularly.

Engaging in training or workshops focused on leadership development can further support this journey toward enhanced self-awareness. These programs often provide tools for introspection and strategies for addressing personal blind spots while fostering an environment of peer learning.

Ultimately, the more you understand yourself as a leader, the better equipped you'll be to lead others effectively. Self-awareness lays the foundation for personal growth and sets the stage for impactful leadership that resonates with team members.

Are You Ready to Challenge Yourself Further?

Understanding Self-Improvement

Self-improvement is not a one-time event; it's an ongoing process that requires intentionality and effort. To truly grow as a leader, you need to cultivate habits that support your development. This involves setting clear goals, seeking feedback, and being open to new experiences. **Establishing specific, measurable objectives** allows you to track your progress and understand what works for you and what doesn't. Instead of vague aspirations like "becoming a better leader," focus on actionable steps such as improving communication skills or enhancing decision-making abilities.

Seeking Feedback

Feedback is a critical component of self-improvement. It provides an external perspective that can highlight blind spots you may not see on your own. **Soliciting constructive criticism from peers and mentors** can be incredibly valuable. It creates opportunities for dialogue about your strengths and areas needing attention. Make it a habit to ask for feedback regularly rather than waiting for formal reviews or performance evaluations. This approach shows that you are committed to growth and willing to adapt based on insights from others.

Embracing New Experiences

Another effective strategy for personal growth is *embracing new experiences*. This doesn't mean stepping completely out of your comfort zone every time; rather, it involves taking calculated risks that push your boundaries just enough to foster development. For instance, if public speaking terrifies you, consider joining a local Toastmasters club or volunteering to lead small meetings at work. These incremental challenges build confidence over time and improve your leadership capabilities without overwhelming you.

The Power of Reflection

Reflection plays a crucial role in continuous improvement. Taking time to think about your experiences allows you to identify lessons learned and areas for future focus. **Journaling can be an excellent tool** for this purpose. Write down your daily experiences, thoughts on leadership challenges, and reflections on feedback received. This practice not only enhances self-awareness but also serves as a record of your journey that can motivate you when facing setbacks.

Building a Support Network

Surrounding yourself with a supportive network can amplify your growth efforts. Engage with colleagues who inspire you or seek mentors who have the experience you're aiming to acquire. **Building relationships with diverse individuals** can offer fresh perspectives and insights that challenge your thinking patterns, leading to more profound growth opportunities.

Setting Up Accountability

Accountability is essential for maintaining momentum in self-improvement efforts. Share your goals with someone who can check in on your progress—this could be a colleague, mentor, or even a friend outside of work. **Regular check-ins help reinforce commitment** and keep you focused on the path you've chosen for personal development.

Continuous Learning

Lastly, never underestimate the value of continuous learning. Whether through formal education, online courses, or simply reading books related to leadership and personal development, staying informed will equip you with new ideas and strategies applicable to real-life situations. **Prioritize learning as part of your routine**, making it an integral part of how you grow both personally and professionally.

Implementing these strategies will not only enhance self-awareness but also lay the groundwork for sustained personal growth throughout your leadership journey. The path might be challenging at times, but the rewards of becoming a more effective leader are well worth the effort invested in self-improvement initiatives.

Navigating Internal Conflicts

Every leader experiences internal conflicts. These conflicts often stem from competing priorities, differing values, or self-doubt. Recognizing and managing these internal battles is crucial for maintaining focus and motivation. It's important to understand that these conflicts are not signs of weakness; rather, they signal an opportunity for growth and self-discovery.

To effectively manage internal conflicts, start by identifying the source of your struggle. Are you torn between pursuing a bold new initiative and adhering to established protocols? Do you feel pressure from stakeholders while trying to stay true to your vision? Pinpointing the root cause allows you to tackle it head-on rather than letting it fester in the background.

Engaging in reflective practices can be immensely beneficial. Take time to journal your thoughts or meditate on your feelings. This self-reflection can help clarify your values and priorities, providing insight into what truly matters to you as a leader. When you're clear about your core beliefs, it becomes easier to navigate difficult decisions without losing sight of your goals.

Embracing Discomfort

Internal conflicts often bring discomfort. Embrace this discomfort as a natural part of the leadership experience. Instead of avoiding tough conversations or challenging situations, lean into them. **This approach not only builds resilience but also reinforces your commitment to personal growth.** It's through confronting these challenges that you sharpen your leadership skills and develop deeper self-awareness.

When facing an internal conflict, consider discussing it with trusted colleagues or mentors. They can provide valuable perspectives that help illuminate blind spots you might not see on your own. Engaging in open dialogue fosters a supportive environment where ideas can be exchanged freely, reducing feelings of isolation during challenging times.

Setting Clear Intentions

Setting clear intentions is another effective way to manage internal conflict. When you establish specific goals for yourself, it becomes easier to filter out distractions and focus on what truly matters. Define what success looks like for you in both personal and professional contexts. This clarity can serve as a guiding light during tumultuous times.

Moreover, **breaking down larger objectives into smaller, manageable tasks can alleviate the overwhelm** associated with internal conflict. This technique enables you to tackle one issue at a time rather than feeling paralyzed by the enormity of the situation. Celebrate small wins along the way; each step forward is progress toward resolving the underlying conflict.

Maintaining Motivation

Maintaining motivation amidst internal conflict requires intentional effort. Revisit your "why"—the reasons behind your leadership journey—and keep those motivations front and centre in your mind. When challenges arise, remind yourself of the impact you want to make and the legacy you wish to leave behind.

In addition, surrounding yourself with positive influences can help sustain motivation during tough times. Seek out individuals who inspire you and challenge your thinking constructively. Their encouragement can provide the boost needed to navigate through uncertain waters with confidence.

Conclusion: A Lifelong Process

Managing internal conflicts is an ongoing process that demands patience and practice. As you grow in self-awareness and learn more about yourself, these conflicts may evolve but will continue to surface throughout your leadership journey. Recognize that each instance provides a chance for introspection and development.

By actively engaging with your internal conflicts—identifying their sources, embracing discomfort, setting clear intentions, and maintaining motivation—you lay a strong foundation for effective leadership. This process not only enhances personal growth but also equips you with the tools necessary for inspiring others through their own challenges.

As we navigate the journey of leadership, the confrontation with ourselves—our inner strengths and weaknesses—becomes inevitable and essential. Recognizing and understanding these facets not only shapes us into more adept leaders but also propels us toward sustained personal growth and effectiveness. The essence of this chapter hinges on the transformative power of self-awareness and the relentless pursuit of self-improvement.

The Reflective Leader's Pathway

Step 1: Engage in Self-Reflection

Begin your journey by dedicating time for introspection. Reflect on your past roles and the various situations you've handled as a leader. Identify instances of both triumph and challenge. Capture these reflections in a journal, noting the skills that led to successes and the obstacles that pinpointed areas needing enhancement. This practice should be regular, perhaps weekly, allowing about 30 minutes per session to write and review.

Step 2: Seek External Feedback

After you've established a baseline of self-assessment, reach out to peers, mentors, or team members whose opinions you value. Ask pointed questions about how they perceive your leadership style, communication, and decision-making skills. This step is crucial as it opens up perspectives that you might be blind to. Aim for monthly feedback sessions to ensure continuous insight.

Step 3: Analyze Feedback and Reflect

With feedback in hand, compare it against your personal reflections. Look for recurring themes or discrepancies that might reveal new areas of strength or needed improvement. This synthesis of internal and external viewpoints will provide a clearer picture of your leadership landscape.

Step 4: Develop an Action Plan

Translate your insights into an actionable plan. Detail specific strategies to harness your strengths and address your weaknesses. This might involve pursuing additional training, seeking mentorship, or taking on new projects that push you out of your comfort zone. Set clear goals with realistic deadlines to track your progress.

Step 5: Implement Regular Self-Assessment

Make self-assessment a routine practice. Regularly revisit your journal and action plan, perhaps quarterly, to evaluate how well you're meeting your goals and make adjustments as necessary. This ongoing process ensures that your growth as a leader does not stagnate.

Step 6: Embrace a Growth Mindset

Finally, commit to viewing self-awareness and improvement as a perpetual journey. A growth mindset will enable you to treat challenges as opportunities to learn and evolve continuously.

By following these steps, you engage in a dynamic process of growth that not only enhances your leadership skills but also deepens your self-knowledge. This pathway does not promise an easy journey—true growth seldom does—but it offers a fulfilling one where each step forward is a step toward becoming a more effective and enlightened leader.

As we wrap up this chapter, remember that the road to leadership excellence is paved with the stones of self-awareness and relentless self-improvement. Each challenge faced, and each reflection pondered adds depth to your leadership abilities, equipping you to lead with more empathy, clarity, and effectiveness. Engage actively in this journey, for the most formidable opponent and the greatest teacher you will ever encounter in your career is yourself. Embrace this challenge, and watch as you transform not only your leadership but also your life.

Chapter Nine

25 PENNIES TO MOVE FORWARD

Can Resourcefulness Turn Twenty-Five Pennies into a Fortune?

As a child, I learned that twenty-five pennies could take me anywhere—at least as far as Route 17 would go. That bus fare wasn't just a handful of coins; it was my ticket to independence, exploration, and lessons in resourcefulness that shaped the leader I would one day become.

Growing up, I never felt like we were without. My mother worked tirelessly to provide for us, and her hard work ensured we always had what we needed, even if it wasn't always what we wanted. Sure, there were times when we went without cable or, for a stretch, without electricity. But those moments weren't framed as hardships—they were opportunities to adapt, to make do, and to appreciate the value of what we had.

One thing I always understood was the power of pennies. My mother taught me how to make every cent count, and as a young boy, I took that lesson to heart. Those twenty-five pennies weren't just bus fare—they were a tangible reminder of the effort it took to earn them, the decisions they demanded, and the opportunities they unlocked.

Resourcefulness became second nature to me during those bus rides. Every trip requires choices: Should I spend the fare both ways, or could I walk part of the route and save some change? Could I hold on to a few pennies for a treat at the corner store? These small decisions taught me how to prioritize, budget, and think critically—all skills that would later become vital in my career.

As I grew older and stepped into leadership roles, I found that those early lessons in resourcefulness carried over seamlessly. Leadership, especially in operations, is rarely about having everything you need. More often, it's about figuring out how to achieve your goals with limited resources. It's about seeing constraints not as barriers but as opportunities to innovate.

I remember one particular challenge early in my career. We were facing a significant equipment shortage during a critical period in our distribution network. Orders were piling up, and there wasn't room in the budget for expensive rentals. I thought back to those childhood lessons about making the most of what you have and started reaching out to nearby markets, asking if they had any equipment to spare. By coordinating across the region, we developed a sharing plan that solved the problem without additional costs. It wasn't a traditional solution, but it worked—and it reinforced my belief that resourcefulness is often the difference between success and failure.

Growing up, I was thankful for the perspective those twenty-five pennies gave me. They taught me that what you have isn't as important as how you use it. There were moments when the lights were out, and we had to light candles to get through the evening. Those nights weren't dark in my memory—they were warm filled with conversations and connection. It wasn't about what we didn't have; it was about appreciating what we did.

That mindset of gratitude and adaptability has shaped how I approach leadership. When resources are tight, I don't focus on what's missing—I focus on what's possible. Whether it's stretching a lean budget, managing a short-staffed team, or finding creative ways to meet customer demands, resourcefulness is the skill that bridges the gap between constraints and outcomes.

Leadership is full of moments that test your ability to adapt. Just like those days when we made it work without cable or electricity, operations often demand quick thinking and resilience. I've been in situations where processes broke down, deadlines loomed, and customers were waiting. Those moments aren't for panic—they're for problem-solving. And the best problem-solvers are those who can see the potential in what they have, no matter how limited it may seem.

Resourcefulness also means understanding people. As a kid, I'd watch how my mother stretched every dollar to make ends meet, not just for the sake of the bills but to ensure I never felt the weight of what we didn't have. She showed me that resourcefulness isn't just about managing things—it's about caring for people. That lesson has stayed with me throughout my career.

In leadership, it's not enough to manage resources efficiently; you have to invest in your people, ensuring they feel supported and valued, even in tough times. I've led teams through challenging periods where raises weren't possible, or budgets were slashed. By being transparent, involving the team in problem-solving, and finding non-monetary ways to show appreciation, we've been able to maintain morale and achieve remarkable results.

Twenty-five pennies might not seem like much, but they taught me lessons that money can't buy. They taught me to prioritize, to adapt, and to make the most of what I had. They taught me to appreciate the effort behind every resource, whether it was a handful of change or a team of hardworking individuals.

Looking back, I realize that those early lessons weren't just about survival—they were about learning to thrive under any circumstances. Leadership, at its heart, is about finding opportunities in constraints, creating solutions where others see problems, and making sure the people around you feel empowered to do the same.

So, can resourcefulness turn twenty-five pennies into a fortune? Maybe not in the literal sense, but the mindset it cultivates—the creativity, resilience, and appreciation for what you have—can lead to success far greater than money. Because at the end of the day, leadership isn't about the resources you have—it's about how you use them to make a lasting impact.

Resourcefulness isn't about having everything—it's about seeing the potential in what you already have and turning it into more than anyone thought possible." – Quentin J. Walker

Unleashing Potential with Every Penny

In a world where resources often seem limited, and challenges loom large, the true test of leadership is not merely in doing more with less but in creatively maximizing what one already possesses. Leadership isn't just about having access to abundant resources; it's about optimizing what you have, no matter how small, to forge ahead. This chapter delves into the core of resourcefulness—a trait indispensable for leaders navigating the challenging terrains of their professional and personal lives.

The Essence of Resourcefulness

Imagine you're at the helm of a startup or leading a new project with a tight budget. Here, every decision counts, and every small contribution has the potential to make or break your path forward. It's not just about stretching dollars but stretching ideas; it's about seeing potential where others see paucity. The ability to look beyond conventional solutions and find innovative ways to utilize available resources can set a leader apart. This chapter will explore **how effective leaders harness creativity and resourcefulness** to solve problems and achieve goals.

The Art of Managing Scarce Resources

Effective resource management is pivotal for any leader aiming to maximize impact with limited inputs. This entails not only careful planning and strategic allocation but also a continual assessment of how resources are utilized. Leaders must learn to assess, adapt, and act swiftly yet judiciously to ensure that every effort counts toward achieving the larger objectives. We'll dissect strategies that help in optimizing resources, ensuring that nothing goes to waste—be it time, money, or talent.

Small Contributions Matter

There's profound strength in recognizing and valuing small contributions within any team or project. Often, it's the aggregation of these small inputs that leads to substantial outcomes. This chapter highlights *why appreciating these minute details* is crucial for leadership success. By fostering an environment where every penny and every moment are valued, leaders can inspire their teams to contribute more effectively and efficiently.

Leadership demands vision, but equally, it requires an appreciation for the granular aspects of execution—the nuts and bolts that hold everything together. Whether it's capitalizing on unexpected opportunities or leveraging overlooked assets, the capacity to make significant advances with seemingly insignificant resources is what often defines transformative leadership.

The insights offered here aim not just to inspire but also to equip you with practical skills to turn constraints into launching pads for innovation and growth. Through real-life examples and actionable advice, we will uncover how leaders can cultivate a mindset that views every challenge as an opportunity for creativity.

Engaging with this narrative will prepare you to not only manage resources wisely but also value each small step towards your larger goal. In doing so, you become a leader who not only drives progress but also inspires it in others—turning every penny into a stepping stone towards success.

Leadership in today's fast-paced environment requires more than just vision and authority; it demands **resourcefulness**. Young leaders often find themselves in situations where resources are limited, yet expectations remain high. This reality can be daunting, but understanding how to leverage creativity and resourcefulness can turn challenges into opportunities. By fostering a mindset that prioritizes innovative solutions, leaders can inspire their teams and drive progress even when the odds seem stacked against them.

Resourcefulness is not merely about making do with what you have; it's about **seeing potential where others see obstacles**. It involves looking at a problem from multiple angles, brainstorming unconventional solutions, and encouraging a culture of experimentation within the team. When leaders exhibit this quality, they create an environment where team members feel empowered to share their ideas without fear of failure. This not only boosts morale but also enhances collaboration as diverse perspectives come together to tackle issues.

Imagine a team tasked with completing a project under tight constraints. Rather than getting bogged down by limitations, a resourceful leader would gather the group and encourage creative thinking sessions. These meetings can lead to unexpected breakthroughs, such as utilizing existing tools in novel ways or reallocating tasks based on individual strengths. Such approaches demonstrate that resourcefulness is about **optimizing available assets**, no matter how scarce they may appear.

Moreover, **creative problem-solving** extends beyond immediate challenges. It cultivates resilience within the team. When young leaders model this behaviour, they teach their teams to embrace uncertainty and adapt quickly to changing circumstances. Resilience becomes part of the organizational culture, making everyone more equipped to handle future difficulties. This adaptability is vital as it fosters long-term sustainability in any venture.

Another aspect of resourcefulness is **the ability to prioritize effectively**. With limited resources, leaders must identify what truly matters and align efforts accordingly. This process often involves tough decisions about where to allocate time and energy for maximum impact. By focusing on high-priority tasks that align with the broader vision, leaders can ensure that their limited resources yield substantial results.

It's essential for young leaders to remember that being resourceful does not mean working harder; it means working smarter. This could involve harnessing technology to automate repetitive tasks or seeking partnerships that expand capabilities without requiring additional funding. The goal is always to find efficient pathways that lead towards achieving objectives while maximizing every penny spent— much like transforming 25 pennies into something greater.

Finally, embracing resourcefulness instils confidence in both leaders and their teams. When people see that challenges can be overcome through innovation and collaboration, they become more engaged and motivated. They begin to understand that every small contribution counts towards larger goals—a fundamental lesson for any young leader embarking on their journey.

What Creative Solutions Will You Discover Next?

The Importance of Resource Management

Effective resource management is a fundamental skill for any leader, especially for those stepping into new roles. When resources are limited, the challenge lies in making the most of what you have. This isn't just about financial resources; it encompasses time, human capital, and even emotional energy. Young leaders often find themselves in situations where they need to achieve significant outcomes without the luxury of ample resources. Understanding how to maximize these inputs is essential for success.

Prioritizing tasks becomes crucial when managing limited resources. Not all tasks hold equal weight in terms of impact. Leaders must assess which activities drive the most value and focus on those first. This might mean tackling high-impact projects that align closely with organizational goals or addressing issues that could derail progress if left unattended. By prioritizing effectively, leaders can ensure that their efforts yield the greatest return on investment, even when operating under constraints.

Embracing Creativity

Resource limitations often breed creativity. When faced with challenges, young leaders can tap into their innovative potential to devise unique solutions. Think about it: when traditional methods are unavailable or impractical, leaders are pushed to explore alternative routes. This can lead to fresh ideas and novel approaches that not only solve immediate problems but also foster a culture of innovation within teams. Encouraging team members to brainstorm and collaborate can generate a wealth of ideas, transforming constraints into opportunities.

Networking and leveraging existing relationships also play a pivotal role in effective resource management. Building strong connections within your industry can provide access to shared resources, mentorship, or even partnerships that enhance capabilities without requiring additional expenditure. Engaging with others who have faced similar challenges can offer insights and strategies that may not be apparent from an isolated perspective.

Setting Clear Goals

Establishing clear goals is another cornerstone of effective resource management. Leaders should define specific objectives that align with their vision while being realistic about what can be achieved given available resources. These goals serve as a guiding light for decision-making and help maintain focus amidst distractions and competing priorities. Clear objectives also enable leaders to track progress and make adjustments as necessary, ensuring that their efforts remain aligned with broader organizational aims.

In addition to setting goals, **measuring outcomes** is vital for assessing the effectiveness of resource allocation. Leaders should implement metrics that allow them to evaluate how well they're utilizing their limited resources over time. Whether it's through feedback loops or performance indicators, understanding what works—and what doesn't—provides invaluable data for future decision-making.

Cultivating a Resourceful Mindset

Finally, cultivating a resourceful mindset within teams encourages everyone to think creatively about their contributions. When team members recognize the importance of valuing every input—whether it's a small idea or a minor investment—they become more engaged and proactive in finding solutions. Leaders should foster an environment where experimentation is welcomed, and failure is viewed as a learning opportunity rather than a setback.

This mindset shift not only enhances individual contributions but also strengthens team cohesion as everyone works together towards common goals with limited means. When each person feels empowered to contribute their unique strengths, it amplifies collective problem-solving capabilities.

By mastering effective resource management techniques, young leaders can navigate the complexities of their roles more confidently. Adopting these practices will not only help them maximize outputs despite limited inputs but also lay the groundwork for future successes as they continue on their leadership journey.

Small Contributions, Big Impact

Every leader knows that achieving significant goals often requires rallying the collective efforts of a team. It's easy to overlook the importance of small contributions in this process. However, recognizing and valuing each member's input can lead to remarkable outcomes. When young leaders learn to appreciate even the smallest efforts, they create an environment where everyone feels empowered to contribute. This collective spirit not only boosts morale but also enhances creativity and innovation.

Consider a community garden as an example. Each individual may only contribute a few seeds or a handful of soil, but when combined, these small contributions can transform a barren plot into a flourishing space. Similarly, in leadership, every idea shared and every task completed—no matter how minor—adds to the overall success of the project. **Fostering a culture that values these small contributions encourages team members to engage actively and take ownership of their roles**.

Cultivating Collaboration

Collaboration is at the heart of effective leadership. When leaders actively encourage collaboration, they allow diverse perspectives to flourish. This openness creates a breeding ground for innovative ideas that can stem from seemingly insignificant contributions. For instance, during brainstorming sessions, it's essential for leaders to remind their teams that no idea is too small or trivial. Even the most basic suggestion can spark inspiration in others and lead to breakthroughs that propel projects forward.

Moreover, acknowledging these contributions fosters trust within the team. When individuals feel valued for their input, they are more likely to share their thoughts freely in the future. This trust builds stronger relationships among team members and cultivates an atmosphere where people are motivated to work together towards shared objectives. **Leaders should celebrate small wins and recognize individual efforts publicly,** reinforcing this culture of appreciation.

Shifting Perspectives on Contribution

It's crucial for leaders to shift their perspective on what constitutes valuable input. Often, teams focus heavily on large milestones while neglecting the smaller steps that lead up to them. By emphasizing the importance of incremental progress, young leaders can reshape how their teams view success. Each small contribution is a stepping stone toward achieving larger goals.

Encouraging this mindset can also help alleviate feelings of overwhelm among team members who may be daunted by big tasks ahead. When individuals see how their minor roles fit into the bigger picture, they gain clarity and motivation to push forward. **This approach emphasizes that every effort counts**, making it easier for everyone involved to stay focused and engaged.

Real-Life Examples

Real-life examples can effectively illustrate how small contributions lead to substantial achievements. Think about successful movements in history—many began with individual actions that collectively created significant change. Leaders like Martin Luther King Jr., who mobilized communities through simple acts of participation, demonstrate how grassroots efforts can escalate into powerful movements.

In businesses, too, many startups have thrived on the foundational ideas contributed by early employees or customers. These initial insights often shape the trajectory of a company's growth. Highlighting such examples inspires young leaders by showing them that *every action counts*, no matter how seemingly insignificant it may appear at first glance.

Encouraging Ownership

Encouraging ownership among team members is another way to leverage small contributions effectively. When individuals take responsibility for their tasks, they become more invested in outcomes. Young leaders should cultivate an environment where team members feel comfortable owning their roles and sharing their ideas without fear of judgment.

This sense of ownership transforms small contributions into essential building blocks for larger projects or initiatives. As individuals recognize their impact on collective success, they become more engaged and proactive in seeking opportunities for improvement within their workspaces.

Conclusion: The Power of Appreciation

Appreciating small contributions is not merely an act of acknowledgement; it's an empowering practice that strengthens teamwork and fosters innovation. Young leaders must remember that every effort matters in achieving broader objectives and creating lasting change within their organizations.

By instilling this mindset among team members, leaders create spaces where creativity flourishes, and collaboration thrives—a critical component for any successful venture moving forward. In doing so, they ensure that all voices are heard and valued, ultimately leading to more significant achievements together as a cohesive unit ready to tackle any challenge ahead.

As we wrap up our discussion, let's reflect on the essential skills of resourcefulness and creative problem-solving that we've explored. The ability to maximize limited resources is not just a skill but a leadership imperative. It demands a keen appreciation for every small contribution and the foresight to manage resources judiciously. These are not just strategies; they are foundational principles that can guide you through the complexities of leadership.

Resourcefulness is about seeing beyond the obvious, finding value in the overlooked, and transforming the minimal into the substantial. Think of it as the art of turning 25 pennies into a dollar—a metaphor for making the most of what you have. This mindset propels leaders to innovate and achieve more with less, which is crucial in today's ever-changing business landscape.

Effective resource management, on the other hand, is about orchestrating all parts, big and small, towards a unified goal. It's like directing an orchestra where every note, no matter how subtle, contributes to the beauty of the symphony. This skill ensures that no resource, no matter how minor it may seem, is wasted. The efficiency gained here not only boosts productivity but also fosters a culture of mindfulness and appreciation among team members.

Moreover, recognizing and valuing small contributions can significantly enhance team morale and engagement. When leaders acknowledge the minor yet critical inputs from their teams, it builds a sense of ownership and pride in the work. This is crucial for nurturing a motivated and committed workforce.

As we move forward, remember that these lessons are not just applicable to managing projects or running companies. They are vital in navigating the myriad challenges and opportunities you will encounter on your leadership journey. Each small step taken with intention and understanding can lead to substantial progress and, ultimately, to achieving greater success.

Keep these principles in mind as you continue to steer through your path in leadership. Embrace resourcefulness, manage with precision, and always value every contribution, no matter how small. These practices will not only advance your professional objectives but also enrich your personal growth as a leader. Let these ideas be your guide as you continue to drive forward, making each penny count towards your larger goals.

Chapter Ten

PLAY THE LONG GAME, BUT KEEP IT FRESH

Early morning stillness was something I have always appreciated. It reminded me of those quiet moments I had as a child, standing on the sidewalk waiting for the bus. Back then, the world felt both vast and small, like I was standing at the edge of something big but tethered to the safety of home. Looking back, those moments taught me something essential about leadership: courage doesn't come all at once. It's built piece by piece, forged in the choices we make when no one else is watching.

I remember one particular day when I was about seven years old. I'd begged my mother to let me walk to the store on my own. The store wasn't far, but it felt like a world away to me then—a place where I could test my independence. She hesitated but eventually handed me a few dollars, gave me clear instructions, and watched from the door as I walked off.

That short journey was exhilarating. Every step felt like an adventure, every crack in the sidewalk a decision point. By the time I returned, with a loaf of bread in one hand and a sense of accomplishment in the other, something had shifted inside me.

That little trip taught me about risk, responsibility, and the satisfaction of stepping into the unknown.

Years later, as I found myself leading teams and navigating complex challenges, I realized that the courage I built on those short walks formed the foundation of the resilience I needed to make tough decisions. Leadership often feels like that solo trek—stepping out with a mix of preparation and uncertainty, hoping that your instincts and lessons from the past will guide you.

In operations, playing the long game is a critical skill. It's about seeing beyond the immediate crisis and focusing on the bigger picture. But here's the catch: you can't afford to let the long game get stale. Keeping it fresh—bringing new ideas, energy, and adaptability to the table—is what separates good leaders from great ones.

I once faced a situation where our processes had grown outdated. They worked, but just barely. Everyone was comfortable with the status quo, but I could see the cracks forming. If we didn't adapt, we'd fall behind. The solution I proposed wasn't easy or popular—it required significant investment and a temporary dip in productivity. But I knew it was the right move for the long term.

Convincing the team wasn't easy. People resist change, especially when what they have seems to work well enough. However, leadership isn't about avoiding conflict or staying in one's comfort zone. It's about having the courage to make decisions that push the team—and the organization—forward.

That courage, I believe, starts in childhood. It's built in those moments when you're forced to rely on yourself, to navigate unfamiliar territory, and to trust that you'll figure it out. For me, those moments didn't just happen on the way to the store—they happened at home, too.

Growing up, I was responsible for more than most kids my age. Whether it was handling chores, cooking dinner, or managing my own homework, I had to step up and figure things out. Those experiences weren't just about getting things done; they were about building the confidence to take ownership, even when I wasn't sure I had all the answers.

In leadership, that sense of ownership is everything. It's what gives you the courage to step into a boardroom and pitch a bold new idea, knowing it might not land. It's what helps you face setbacks with resilience, trusting that you'll find a way through.

But courage alone isn't enough. Playing the long game requires vision, adaptability, and the ability to keep things fresh. It's not about sticking rigidly to a plan—it's about being open to new possibilities and finding ways to keep your team engaged and inspired.

I think about the teams I've led through periods of change. Some of those changes were planned, while others were thrown at us unexpectedly. In both cases, the key to success was keeping the team focused on the long-term goal while staying flexible enough to adjust along the way.

One of the best lessons I've learned is that innovation often comes from the most unexpected places. During one particularly challenging process overhaul, a junior team member suggested an idea I hadn't considered. At first, I dismissed it, thinking it was too simple to work. But as I gave it more thought, I realized it was exactly what we needed. That experience taught me to stay open, to keep listening, and to remember that fresh perspectives can bring new life to even the most established plans.

Courage isn't just about big, dramatic decisions. It's about the small, everyday choices that build momentum. It's about staying consistent in your values while being willing to adapt your approach.

That's what playing the long game is all about. It's about staying committed to the big picture while keeping things fresh enough to stay relevant. It's about finding the balance between stability and innovation, between sticking to your principles and embracing change.

Looking back, I realize that those early walks to the store weren't just errands—they were lessons. They taught me how to trust myself, how to face uncertainty, and how to take small risks that lead to big rewards.

As leaders, we need to remember that courage doesn't come all at once. It's built over time through the choices we make and the challenges we face. And just like those walks, leadership is a journey—one that requires us to play the long game while staying open to new possibilities along the way.

"Courage isn't born in a single moment—it's built step by step, in the small risks we take and the lessons we learn along the way. True leadership is about balancing the patience to play the long game with the creativity to keep it fresh." – Quentin J.

Walker

From Resilience to Relevance: Leading with Agility and Vision

Leadership isn't just about steering the ship through calm waters; it's about being prepared to navigate through storms, chart new paths, and continually adapt to changing seas. This chapter delves into the intricate balance of maintaining long-term goals while staying agile enough to tackle immediate challenges and opportunities that arise unexpectedly.

Imagine leadership as a journey where the road ahead is not always clear, and sometimes you must forge your own path. The essence of effective leadership lies in **balancing strategic foresight with the flexibility** to seize opportunities as they come. This doesn't just happen—it requires a mindset that blends resilience, courage, and innovative thinking.

The Dual Demands of Leadership

At the heart of strategic leadership is the ability to think long-term. Leaders must envision their destination years before they reach it, plotting a course that considers potential pitfalls and opportunities. However, the reality of any journey includes unexpected detours and sudden obstacles. Here lies the critical skill: **adapting swiftly without losing sight of the ultimate goal**.

Adaptation and Evolution: Key Leadership Skills

Changing circumstances often demand that leaders adjust their styles—from authoritative to delegative, from hands-on to purely inspirational—depending on what will best move the team forward. *Flexibility in leadership style* is not about inconsistency; it's about being attuned to the needs of the moment while keeping your team aligned with long-term objectives.

Leaders today face an unprecedented pace of change. Technology evolves rapidly, consumer behaviours shift, and entire industries transform overnight. In this environment, *leaders must cultivate a culture of innovation* within their organizations. This means encouraging risk-taking within safe boundaries and promoting a mindset where every challenge is viewed as an opportunity for growth.

Continuous Innovation: The Lifeline of Progress

Maintaining relevance in a fast-paced world requires a commitment to continuous improvement and innovation. It's about fostering an environment where new ideas are welcomed and tested and where failures are seen as stepping stones to success. This approach not only keeps the organization ahead of curves but also embeds a crucial trait in its culture: resilience.

Resilience is often born from facing difficult situations head-on—just as navigating challenging routes can teach invaluable lessons about perseverance and adaptability. Leaders who embrace these experiences grow their capacity to handle future uncertainties more effectively.

Why Leaders Must Play the Long Game

Finally, playing the long game involves preparing yourself and your organization for future challenges by building robust systems, nurturing talent, and creating sustainable growth strategies. It's about understanding that true success is measured not just by immediate achievements but by **long-term impact**—on your industry, on society, and on the lives of those connected to your organization.

This chapter sets out to explore how leaders can maintain their relevance and drive progress by balancing strategic long-term planning with innovative responses to immediate challenges. Through this balance, leaders not only navigate but also shape their journey towards success with resilience and adaptability at their core.

Leadership often requires a balance between long-term vision and short-term action. While having a clear strategic plan is essential for guiding a team toward future goals, the ability to seize immediate opportunities can be just as crucial. A leader who solely focuses on the distant horizon may miss out on valuable chances that arise at the moment. On the other hand, someone who reacts impulsively without a clear direction can lead their team into chaos. Finding that sweet spot between these two approaches is key to effective leadership.

In practice, this balance means taking the time to establish a **vision** while remaining open to unexpected opportunities. For instance, consider a team launching a new product. The long-term strategy may involve extensive market research and development timelines. However, if a competitor announces an unexpected release or market demand shifts suddenly, being able to pivot quickly becomes invaluable. Leaders need to remain vigilant and adaptable, ready to integrate these changing circumstances into their planning.

Building this adaptability starts with cultivating an environment where team members feel empowered to act. Encourage them to bring forth ideas and solutions without waiting for explicit instructions. When team members are engaged and proactive, they naturally contribute to both the strategic plan and immediate actions that can enhance success. This collaborative approach helps create resilience within the team as everyone learns to navigate uncertainty together.

To effectively balance strategic planning with opportunistic actions, leaders should also embrace **flexibility** in their thinking. This doesn't mean abandoning long-term goals; rather, it involves re-evaluating those goals in light of new information or changing contexts. It's about asking questions like: *How does this new opportunity align with our vision? What adjustments need to be made?* By fostering a mindset of continuous learning and adaptation, leaders can ensure that their teams stay relevant and responsive.

Communication plays a critical role in this dynamic as well. Keeping everyone informed about both the long-term objectives and any immediate changes helps maintain alignment among team members. Transparent discussions about what opportunities arise and how they fit into the overall strategy can build trust and encourage collaboration. This clarity allows teams to act swiftly while still keeping sight of their overarching goals.

Another important aspect is measurement. Setting clear metrics for success ensures that leaders can evaluate both short-term results and long-term progress effectively. When leaders know how to measure outcomes from immediate actions against strategic goals, they can make informed decisions about where to invest resources next.

Ultimately, balancing strategic long-term planning with immediate opportunistic actions is not just about managing tasks; it's about developing a resilient leadership style that thrives in uncertainty. Leaders who master this balance will not only guide their teams through challenges but also inspire confidence and adaptability in those they lead.

Are You Ready to Adapt Your Leadership Style?

Understanding Leadership Flexibility

Leadership is not a one-size-fits-all approach. The most effective leaders are those who can adapt their styles to meet the changing needs of their teams and the challenges they face. **The ability to pivot and adjust your leadership style in response to different situations is crucial for success.** A rigid approach can lead to stagnation, while flexibility fosters growth and innovation.

Consider a leader managing a diverse team with varying skill sets and personalities. **An adaptable leader recognizes that what works for one group member may not resonate with another.** By tailoring their approach—whether through motivation, delegation, or communication—they create an environment where everyone feels valued and empowered to contribute. This personalization enhances team cohesion and drives collective success.

Responding to Change

In today's fast-paced world, change is the only constant. Leaders must be prepared to respond swiftly to new challenges, whether they're shifts in market trends, technological advancements, or evolving team dynamics. **The capacity to adjust leadership styles based on these changes can mean the difference between thriving and merely surviving.** For instance, during a crisis, a more directive style may be necessary to provide clarity and direction. Conversely, during periods of stability and growth, a collaborative style might foster creativity and innovation.

Being attuned to the pulse of your team allows you to implement changes effectively. Regular check-ins, feedback sessions, and open lines of communication will help you gauge how well your current leadership approach resonates with your team members. **Leaders who actively seek input from their teams are better equipped to make informed adjustments that reflect the group's evolving needs.**

Embracing Diverse Perspectives

Adaptability also involves embracing diverse perspectives within your team. Each member brings unique experiences and insights that can enrich decision-making processes. **By encouraging open dialogue and valuing contributions from all team members, leaders can cultivate an inclusive atmosphere that thrives on collaboration.** This not only fosters innovation but also helps identify potential pitfalls that might go unnoticed in a more homogeneous environment.

Leaders should practice active listening—truly hearing what team members have to say rather than simply waiting for their turn to speak. When individuals feel heard, they are more likely to share ideas openly and contribute meaningfully to discussions. This culture of respect and appreciation builds trust among team members, enabling smoother transitions when leadership styles need adjusting.

Learning from Experience

Another key aspect of adapting leadership styles is learning from past experiences—both successes and failures. Reflecting on what strategies worked well in previous situations can inform future decisions while acknowledging missteps provide invaluable lessons for growth. **Effective leaders regularly assess their performance and seek opportunities for improvement** through self-evaluation or by soliciting feedback from others.

This commitment to continual learning not only enhances a leader's adaptability but also sets an example for their team. When leaders demonstrate a willingness to evolve based on experience, they encourage others to adopt a similar mindset, fostering a culture of resilience where everyone feels empowered to take risks.

The Role of Emotional Intelligence

A leader's emotional intelligence plays a significant role in adaptability as well. Understanding one's emotions—and recognizing how they impact others—is essential when navigating complex interpersonal dynamics. **Leaders who exhibit high emotional intelligence are better equipped to adjust their approaches according to the emotional climate of their teams**.

Being aware of when tensions rise, or morale dips allows leaders to step in with empathy or encouragement as needed. Whether it's offering support during stressful times or celebrating small wins during challenging projects, tuning into the emotional state of the team enables leaders to pivot effectively without losing momentum.

Building Resilience Through Adaptation

Adapting leadership styles does not just help navigate immediate challenges; it builds resilience within teams as well. When teams see their leaders adeptly handling change, they feel more confident in facing uncertainties themselves. **This shared sense of resilience fosters an environment where individuals are willing to step outside their comfort zones**, knowing they have strong support guiding them through uncharted territories.

Encouraging this mindset will ultimately shape future leaders within your organization who are not only capable but also eager to embrace change as an opportunity for growth rather than an obstacle.

Cultivating Continuous Improvement

Finally, adaptability should be viewed as part of a broader commitment to continuous improvement within leadership practice itself. As new situations arise and trends shift over time, leaders must remain open-minded about incorporating new techniques or strategies into their repertoire. This ongoing development ensures that leaders are well-prepared for whatever challenges lie ahead while keeping their teams engaged and motivated along the way.

By fostering an adaptable leadership style rooted in understanding context, valuing diversity, learning from experience, leveraging emotional intelligence, building resilience, and committing to continuous improvement—leaders can confidently steer their organizations toward success amid uncertainty.

Embracing Change as a Leader

In today's fast-paced world, leaders are constantly faced with the challenge of remaining relevant. The only way to navigate this landscape is through continuous innovation and flexibility. **This means being open to change**, actively seeking new ideas, and adapting strategies to meet the evolving needs of your team and organization. Recognizing that change is not just inevitable, but also an opportunity for growth can transform how you lead.

Innovation doesn't always mean reinventing the wheel. Often, it's about refining existing processes or introducing small adjustments that can yield significant results. Encourage your team to share their insights and creative solutions. When individuals feel empowered to contribute, they're more likely to invest in the success of initiatives. This collaborative environment fosters a culture of innovation where everyone is aligned toward common goals.

Flexibility goes hand in hand with innovation. Leaders must be prepared to pivot when necessary, whether due to shifting market demands, unexpected challenges, or new opportunities on the horizon. This adaptability requires a mindset that embraces uncertainty rather than shies away from it. **As a leader, demonstrating this agility can inspire your team** to adopt a similar approach in their work. When they see you responding positively to change, it encourages them to do the same.

In practical terms, maintaining relevance involves staying informed about industry trends and technological advancements. Regularly assess your strategies and tools—are they still effective? Are there emerging technologies or practices that could enhance productivity? Engaging in ongoing education and professional development helps ensure that you're equipped with the latest knowledge and skills required for effective leadership.

Another crucial aspect of maintaining relevance is understanding your audience—the people you lead. Their needs and expectations may shift over time; therefore, continuous feedback loops are essential. Encourage open communication channels where team members can voice their opinions and experiences. **Actively listening to your team not only builds trust but also provides valuable insights into how you can adapt your leadership style** and strategies.

Don't forget the importance of experimentation in fostering innovation. While it's essential to have a strategic plan, allow room for trial and error. Implement pilot projects or brainstorming sessions where unconventional ideas can be explored without fear of failure. This approach not only cultivates creativity but also reinforces the idea that learning from mistakes is an integral part of growth.

Ultimately, maintaining relevance as a leader requires a balance between vision and action. **Set clear long-term goals** but remain agile enough to seize immediate opportunities as they arise. This dual focus empowers you to guide your team effectively while adapting to changing circumstances. By embracing both innovation and flexibility, you'll cultivate an environment where resilience thrives.

In summary, continuous innovation and flexibility are vital components of effective leadership in today's dynamic landscape. By encouraging creativity within your team, being adaptable in the face of change, staying informed about industry trends, engaging in ongoing learning, fostering open communication, embracing experimentation, and balancing vision with action, you will position yourself—and your organization—for sustained success in an ever-evolving world.

Throughout this discussion, we've navigated the delicate balance between long-term strategic planning and seizing immediate opportunities. This dual approach is not just a strategy; it's a necessary dance in leadership. The ability to adapt your leadership style in response to evolving circumstances isn't just beneficial—it's imperative for survival and relevance in today's fast-paced world.

Remember, the essence of leadership lies in resilience—the capacity to confront the unknown with courage. Just as a young child learns to navigate complex environments, leaders must embrace challenges and uncertainties with a proactive mindset. This is not about reckless risk-taking; it's about calculated courage, where innovation and flexibility are your best tools.

Continuous innovation keeps your strategies fresh and effective. It's akin to updating a map during a long journey; what worked yesterday may not be the best route today. By staying flexible, you ensure that your leadership remains relevant and impactful, no matter how the terrain changes.

To truly play the long game effectively, integrate these lessons into your daily leadership practice:

- **Balance** is crucial. Just as a ship captain adjusts the sails to meet the changing winds, so must you adjust your strategies between long-term goals and short-term realities.

- **Adaptability** in leadership styles is not just about changing tactics but also about understanding and responding to the needs of your team and the demands of the situation.

- **Innovation** should be continuous. Like breathing, it's not something you can do just once and forget about; it needs to become a part of your leadership DNA.

As we move forward, let these principles guide you. They are not merely strategies but essential components of a robust leadership style that thrives on change and uncertainty. Equip yourself with these tools, and you'll find that navigating the complex world of leadership is not just about enduring but excelling.

By fostering a culture of resilience, adaptability, and innovation, you set the stage for sustained success and lasting impact. Let's keep steering towards that horizon with confidence and anticipation for the opportunities it brings.

Chapter Eleven

PURPOSE IN EVERY STEP

Can Long-Term Vision Coexist with Immediate Action?

The hum of activity in a bustling operation is a constant reminder of the balancing act leaders face every day. It's a blend of looking ahead to ensure long-term sustainability while tackling the urgent needs that demand immediate attention. For me, this tension has always felt familiar, rooted in the early lessons of navigating challenges with limited resources.

I vividly remember a moment from a role in operations, managing a distribution centre during peak season. The goal was clear: maintain productivity and service levels while preparing for an overhaul in processes that would set us up for long-term success. On the surface, these goals seemed to coexist, but in practice, they often clashed.

Every day brought immediate fires to put out—trucks delayed, equipment breakdowns, or unexpected spikes in demand. At the same time, the larger project required strategic planning, time, and resources. It felt like I was standing at a crossroads, constantly deciding whether to focus on the task directly in front of me or the bigger picture looming ahead.

Growing up, I learned early on that balance wasn't about choosing one thing over another—it was about learning to manage both. As an only child, I often had responsibilities that required me to prioritize and make decisions quickly. If there were no lights at home that evening, I'd focus on how to manage homework by candlelight while thinking about how to help my mother plan for the next day. It wasn't a matter of either/or; it was about making both work.

Leadership, I've found, operates on the same principle. Can you solve the urgent problem while staying committed to the larger vision? Can you lead your team through the immediate crisis without losing sight of the long-term goal? These questions have shaped how I approach decision-making.

One example stands out vividly. During a major operational shift in one of my roles, we were implementing a new inventory system designed to improve accuracy and efficiency. It was a game-changer, but the rollout created immediate pain points—delays, frustration among team members, and mounting customer complaints.

The team's natural inclination was to put the long-term project on hold and fix the immediate issues. However, I knew that pausing the rollout would delay the benefits we desperately needed for the business to thrive in the future. Instead, we focused on addressing the short-term problems creatively. By reallocating resources, providing additional training, and working long hours to stabilize the process, we managed to keep the rollout on track while satisfying our customers.

It wasn't easy, but the experience reinforced an important lesson: long-term vision and immediate action aren't mutually exclusive. They're two sides of the same coin, and great leaders learn how to leverage both.

For me, this balance comes down to one word: priorities. Knowing what matters most at any given moment is critical. In operations, the temptation to constantly chase the next urgent issue can be overwhelming, but without a clear sense of purpose, you risk spinning your wheels without moving forward.

I've found that asking a few simple questions helps guide my decisions:

- **Does this action align with our long-term goals?**

- **What's the cost of not addressing this issue immediately?**

- **How can we adapt without compromising the bigger picture?**

These questions create clarity in moments of chaos, helping me focus on what truly matters.

Another important factor is adaptability. Sometimes, circumstances demand a shift in priorities. During one particularly challenging year, an unexpected labour shortage threw our entire operation into turmoil. My initial instinct was to double down on recruitment efforts to fill the gap, but I quickly realized that would take time we didn't have. Instead, we adapted by streamlining workflows, cross-training team members, and leveraging temporary solutions to keep the operation moving.

That experience taught me that while long-term planning is essential, flexibility is just as important. The ability to pivot in the face of changing circumstances doesn't undermine your vision—it strengthens it.

It's also important to communicate this balance to your team. In one instance, during a major operational restructuring, my team was growing frustrated with the constant juggling of priorities. They felt torn between meeting immediate goals and working on broader initiatives. I realized that I needed to clarify the "why" behind our actions. By explaining how each step—whether short-term or long-term—fits into the bigger picture, I helped them see the value in both.

Leadership isn't just about balancing your own priorities; it's about helping your team do the same. When people understand the purpose behind their work, they're more willing to adapt and push through challenges.

Looking back, I think about those early lessons in childhood—standing in the grocery store aisle with a list and a few crumpled bills, deciding what was most important. It wasn't about having everything; it was about making the best choice with what I had. That same mindset has carried me through my career, reminding me that leadership is rarely about having perfect conditions. It's about making progress with the resources and information available at the moment.

Long-term vision and immediate action don't have to be at odds. In fact, the best leaders find ways to make them work together. They know when to slow down and plan and when to move quickly and adapt. They understand that success isn't about choosing one path over the other—it's about navigating both with confidence and clarity.

So, as you face your own decisions—whether in leadership or in life—ask yourself: How can you play the long game while keeping it fresh? How can you stay true to your vision while meeting the demands of today? The answer lies in finding your balance and having the courage to move forward, one step at a time.

"Leadership is a delicate dance between foresight and immediacy—true mastery lies in steering the present without losing sight of the future." – Quentin J. Walker

How might you find your balance?

Charting the Course: Why Every Step Counts

In the realm of leadership, the ability to merge vision with practicality often determines both personal and organizational success. The journey of leadership is akin to navigating a complex network of roads; each turn and each decision not only influences immediate outcomes but also shapes the path toward long-term goals. This chapter delves into the art of strategic thinking, which allows leaders to play the long game while seizing fresh opportunities that arise along the way.

Understanding Your "Why"

The first step in any meaningful endeavour is understanding why you're embarking on it in the first place. For leaders, identifying this 'why'—both on a personal and professional level—serves as the compass that guides their decisions and actions. It's about connecting with your core values and motivations. When leaders are clear about their purpose, they navigate challenges more effectively and inspire their teams with clarity and conviction.

Aligning Actions with Long-Term Goals

It's one thing to have a vision; it's another to live it out each day through every action and decision. This chapter explores how leaders can ensure that their daily operations are not just reactive tasks but are steps that align with broader strategic objectives. This alignment is crucial not only for maintaining consistency but also for building a legacy.

Infusing Purpose into Routine

Every task, no matter how small, carries the seed of your larger goals. We'll examine how successful leaders instil a sense of purpose in everyday activities, transforming routine operations into opportunities for advancement and learning. This approach not only enhances motivation across teams but also strengthens the collective focus on end goals.

Strategic thinking is more than just a skill—it's a necessary practice that intertwines foresight with adaptability. Leaders who master this are able to balance long-term goals with immediate needs without losing sight of either. They understand that every choice made today shapes the road ahead.

Leadership requires persistence in keeping everyone's eyes on the horizon while ensuring that today's work strongly supports tomorrow's dreams. **It demands adaptability**, recognizing when plans need adjustment due to changing circumstances or new opportunities.

Ultimately, what this chapter sets forth is a blueprint for leadership that is as dynamic as it is thoughtful. By embracing both long-term planning and immediate action, leaders can ensure sustained progress and relevance in a rapidly changing world.

Through engaging insights and actionable strategies, this discussion aims to equip you with the tools to integrate deep purpose into your leadership approach, ensuring that every step you take is measured, meaningful, and aligned with your ultimate objectives. Remember, effective leadership isn't just about where you're going; it's also about how purposefully you get there.

Understanding one's personal and professional "why" is a critical starting point for effective leadership. Leaders who are clear about their motivations can navigate challenges more effectively and inspire those around them. The "why" acts as a compass, guiding decisions and actions while providing a sense of purpose. When leaders articulate their reasons for pursuing specific goals, it becomes easier to align their choices with their core values, ultimately fostering authenticity in their leadership style.

To identify your personal "why," begin with self-reflection. Ask yourself what drives you. What do you care about most deeply? Consider the moments in your life when you felt truly fulfilled or proud. Was it when you helped someone achieve a goal? Or perhaps when you contributed to a project that made a difference? These experiences often reveal underlying passions that can shape your leadership journey. By articulating these values, you gain clarity on what motivates you, which is essential in times of uncertainty.

In the professional realm, defining your "why" also means understanding the broader impact of your role. Consider how your work contributes to the organization's mission or vision. This connection not only enhances your sense of belonging but also reinforces the significance of your contributions. When leaders recognize that their efforts are part of a larger narrative, they become more engaged and committed to driving results.

Furthermore, sharing your "why" with others can strengthen team dynamics. When a leader expresses their motivations clearly, it encourages team members to reflect on their own purposes. This creates an environment where everyone feels empowered to contribute meaningfully. It fosters collaboration and unity as team members align their personal goals with collective objectives.

While identifying your "why" is essential, it's equally important to revisit and refine it regularly. Life circumstances change, and so do our priorities. A leader's journey is not static; it's dynamic and evolving. Regularly assessing your motivations ensures that you remain connected to what truly matters to you and allows for adjustments as needed in response to new challenges or opportunities.

In addition to personal reflection, consider seeking feedback from trusted colleagues or mentors about how they perceive your strengths and motivations. Sometimes, an outside perspective can highlight qualities or passions you may overlook in yourself. This collaborative approach adds richness to your understanding of both your personal and professional "why."

Ultimately, knowing your "why" establishes a foundation for resilience in leadership. When faced with obstacles or setbacks, this clarity can reignite passion and commitment, reminding you why you embarked on this path in the first place. Leaders who possess this inner strength are more likely to navigate storms effectively while maintaining focus on long-term objectives.

As we explore aligning actions with broader goals in the next section, keep in mind that understanding your personal and professional motivations will serve as the bedrock for making impactful decisions and leading effectively.

What Drives You? Discovering Your Purpose Awaits

Understanding the Connection Between Actions and Values

Aligning individual actions with broader goals and values is crucial for effective leadership. When leaders understand the bigger picture, they can make decisions that resonate not only with their objectives but also with the collective vision of their team or organization. This alignment fosters a sense of purpose and direction, allowing everyone involved to work towards common goals. It's about creating a cohesive environment where each team member recognizes their role in the larger mission.

To achieve this alignment, leaders should first clarify their own values. What principles guide your decision-making? Understanding these personal values is foundational because they influence how you lead others. When you communicate your values clearly, it allows your team to see how their contributions fit into the larger context. This clarity helps to motivate individuals as they recognize the significance of their work beyond just day-to-day tasks.

Next, it's essential to engage your team in discussions about organizational goals and values. Regular conversations around these topics create an atmosphere of inclusivity and shared purpose. Encourage team members to express their views on how their roles align with the organization's objectives. This engagement not only empowers individuals but also reinforces a culture of accountability—everyone feels responsible for moving towards shared goals.

Setting measurable objectives is another vital step in aligning actions with values. When leaders establish clear performance metrics that reflect organizational values, it provides a tangible way for teams to measure success. These metrics should be specific, achievable, relevant, and time-bound (SMART). By breaking down broader goals into actionable steps, you create a roadmap that guides daily activities while keeping everyone focused on the ultimate vision.

It's important to recognize that alignment is not a one-time effort; it requires ongoing assessment and adjustment. Leaders should routinely check in with their teams to evaluate whether actions continue to align with goals and values. This could involve soliciting feedback through surveys or informal discussions, allowing for course corrections as needed. Flexibility in this process demonstrates a commitment to continuous improvement and adaptability—qualities essential for long-term success.

Another critical aspect of this alignment process involves celebrating achievements along the way. Recognizing milestones reinforces the connection between individual efforts and organizational success. Celebrations can be small—like acknowledging a job well done during team meetings—or more significant events that highlight major accomplishments. These moments serve as reminders of how collective efforts contribute to broader objectives, boosting morale and motivation.

Encouraging collaboration within teams also plays a vital role in aligning actions with values. When individuals work together towards common goals, it fosters a sense of community and shared responsibility. Collaborative environments thrive on open communication and trust; leaders can facilitate this by modelling transparency in decision-making processes and encouraging diverse perspectives when tackling challenges.

Ultimately, aligning individual actions with broader goals and values creates a powerful synergy within organizations. It transforms leadership from merely directing tasks to inspiring collective action towards meaningful outcomes. As young leaders embrace this approach, they will find themselves not only navigating their own paths effectively but also guiding their teams toward sustained success with clarity and purpose.

Finding Purpose in Daily Actions

Every leader knows that having a clear sense of purpose is crucial for guiding decisions and actions. However, it's easy to get lost in the daily grind and forget why you started in the first place. A strong sense of purpose transforms routine tasks into meaningful contributions. When leaders connect their daily activities to their broader vision, they not only enhance their own motivation but also inspire those around them. It's about making each action count, no matter how small.

To instil this sense of purpose, begin by articulating your core values and goals. What drives you? What impact do you want to have? Write these down. This exercise clarifies your vision and sets a foundation for your daily tasks. **When you can see how your actions align with your long-term aspirations, you're more likely to approach even the most mundane tasks with enthusiasm.**

Connecting the Dots Between Tasks and Vision

Consider how each task you undertake relates to your overarching mission. For example, if your goal is to foster innovation within your team, think about how responding to emails or participating in meetings contributes to that vision. Every interaction can either advance or hinder progress toward your goals. **By consciously linking daily activities to larger objectives, leaders cultivate an environment where every team member understands their role in achieving success.**

Encourage open conversations within your team about how individual contributions support collective goals. Regularly revisiting these connections keeps everyone aligned and motivated. **When**

people understand the "why" behind their tasks, they become more engaged and proactive in their roles—an essential aspect of effective leadership.

Embracing Flexibility While Staying Focused

While it's important to have a clear purpose, adaptability is equally essential in today's fast-paced environment. Opportunities can arise unexpectedly, and leaders must be willing to pivot while keeping their long-term objectives in mind. This balance between staying focused on the end goal and being open to new possibilities fosters resilience.

For instance, if a new project aligns closely with your mission but requires shifting resources from another initiative, evaluate whether the potential benefits outweigh any drawbacks. Adapting doesn't mean abandoning your vision; it means recalibrating your path when necessary. **A flexible approach allows you to seize immediate opportunities without losing sight of long-term goals**.

Developing Daily Routines That Reinforce Purpose

Creating habits that reinforce a sense of purpose can significantly impact daily performance. Start by incorporating brief moments of reflection into your routine—whether it's at the beginning or end of each day—where you assess how your actions align with your vision and values. This practice not only reinforces accountability but also strengthens commitment.

Additionally, share these reflections with your team during regular check-ins or meetings. When everyone engages in this practice together, it builds camaraderie and collective focus on shared objectives. **Establishing routines that prioritize purpose keeps the team energized and aligned**, enhancing overall performance.

Encouraging Team Members to Find Their Why

As a leader, part of your responsibility is helping team members discover their own sense of purpose within the organization. Encourage them to reflect on their values and career aspirations regularly. This might involve one-on-one discussions where you actively listen and guide them toward understanding how they fit into the larger picture.

Offering professional development opportunities that align with individual goals can also nurture this sense of purpose. When employees see a clear connection between personal growth and organizational success, they are more likely to feel invested in both their work and the company's mission.

Measuring Progress Toward Long-Term Goals

Tracking progress is essential for maintaining momentum towards long-term objectives. Establish metrics that allow both you and your team to assess achievements regularly; this helps celebrate small victories while keeping everyone focused on what lies ahead.

Utilizing tools such as performance reviews or project retrospectives can facilitate honest conversations about progress toward goals. **These evaluations provide valuable insights into what works well and what needs adjustment**, ensuring that every step taken contributes meaningfully toward fulfilling the larger vision.

The Ripple Effect of Purposeful Leadership

Ultimately, when leaders instil a sense of purpose in everyday tasks, they create a ripple effect throughout the organization. Team members who understand how their work contributes to a greater cause are more likely to collaborate effectively and support one another towards achieving shared objectives.

By fostering an environment where every action is tied back to meaningful goals, leaders set the stage for sustained engagement and motivation across all levels of their organization—ensuring that everyone feels valued as part of a larger mission while navigating both immediate challenges and long-term aspirations confidently together.

As we draw together the insights from our discussion, it's essential to recognize that the true essence of leadership lies not just in the grand vision but also in the minute steps that lead us there. The journey of leadership is about understanding your profound "why" and aligning it with both immediate tasks and overarching goals. This approach ensures that every action, no matter how small, is imbued with purpose and direction.

Identifying and defining your personal and professional "why" is more than an introspective exercise—it's a foundational step for any leader. By clarifying this, you set a course that resonates deeply with your values and aspirations, making it easier to navigate through challenges and opportunities alike. This clarity not only fuels your motivation but also serves as a beacon for others to follow.

Aligning individual actions and team efforts with broader organizational objectives transforms routine tasks into significant milestones. This alignment is critical as it fosters a cohesive working environment where every team member understands their role in the larger picture. It turns everyday tasks into pieces of a puzzle everyone is eager to complete, enhancing productivity and satisfaction across the board.

Moreover, **instilling a sense of purpose in everyday tasks and long-term plans** makes the journey enjoyable and fulfilling. When team members see how their contributions fit into the wider goals, it boosts morale and drives engagement. This connection between daily work and ultimate objectives makes each step feel valuable and impactful.

We've discussed how strategic thinking involves a delicate balance between immediate actions and long-term planning. It's about playing the long game while staying fresh and adaptable to seize opportunities as they arise. This dynamic approach keeps you relevant and forward-moving, ensuring that your leadership remains effective even as circumstances change.

Remember, the power of a well-defined purpose in leadership cannot be overstated. It transforms visions into realities and turns ordinary opportunities into stepping stones for success. As you continue on your leadership journey, keep these principles in mind. They will not only guide you but also inspire those you lead, creating a legacy of success and fulfilment.

By embracing these concepts, you're not just leading; you're empowering yourself and others to make every step count towards a meaningful and successful journey.

Chapter Twelve

SQUAD GOALS: LIFT AS YOU CLIMB

Can Leadership Truly Be Selfless?

Leadership is often portrayed as selfless—a noble act of putting others before oneself. But as I reflect on my own journey, I've come to realize that the reality is more complex. True leadership isn't about completely sacrificing yourself for the good of others; it's about finding the balance between serving the team and holding yourself accountable for its success. It's about aligning your purpose with the growth and well-being of those you lead.

Growing up, I witnessed selflessness firsthand. My mother, a single parent, worked tirelessly to provide for me. She often put my needs above her own, sacrificing sleep, leisure, and personal ambitions to make sure I had what I needed. At the time, I didn't fully understand the depth of her sacrifices, but as I grew older, I saw the toll it took on her.

Her example taught me an important lesson: selflessness has its limits. If you give everything without taking care of yourself, you risk burnout, resentment, and losing the ability to truly lead effectively. Leadership, I realized, must balance the selfless desire to serve with the practical need to maintain your own strength and clarity.

In operations, the demands on leaders are constant. There are always fires to put out, metrics to meet, and people who need guidance. Early in my career, I thought being a good leader meant always saying "yes"—yes to every request, every challenge, and every opportunity to help. But over time, I learned that this approach wasn't sustainable. Trying to be everything for everyone left me exhausted and ineffective.

The turning point came during a particularly challenging period when my team was stretched thin, and I felt the pressure to step in and take on more than my share. I stayed late every night, picked up tasks that weren't mine, and avoided delegating because I didn't want to burden anyone else. At first, it seemed like the right thing to do—a demonstration of commitment and selflessness. But the cracks began to show. I became short-tempered, less focused, and less available to provide real leadership.

One day, a team member pulled me aside and said, "We appreciate everything you're doing, but we need you to lead, not just work harder than us." That hit me hard. My efforts to be selfless had actually undermined my ability to lead.

From that experience, I learned a valuable truth: leadership isn't about doing everything for your team—it's about empowering them to succeed. That means stepping back, trusting others to take responsibility, and focusing on the bigger picture. It's about serving the team by providing direction, support, and accountability rather than trying to shoulder every burden yourself.

Selflessness in leadership doesn't mean ignoring your own needs. In fact, taking care of yourself is one of the most selfless things you can do as a leader. When you're rested, focused, and clear-headed, you're better equipped to serve your team. It's like the oxygen mask analogy on aeroplanes: you have to secure your own mask first before helping others.

There's also an element of courage in selfless leadership. It's not just about giving—it's about having the humility to admit when you don't have all the answers, the strength to ask for help, and the willingness to make decisions that might not be popular but are necessary for the team's success.

I think back to a time when I had to make a tough call that wasn't well-received. We were facing budget constraints, and I had to reassign resources from one team to another. It wasn't an easy decision, and it caused tension among the affected employees. But it was the right decision for the organization's long-term success.

Afterwards, I took the time to explain the reasoning behind the decision, listen to concerns, and work with those impacted to ensure they felt supported. It wasn't about being liked—it was about doing what was necessary for the greater good while still showing empathy and respect.

That experience reinforced that leadership is often about making sacrifices—not just personal ones but also asking others to adapt or change for the greater good. The key is to approach those moments with transparency, empathy, and a clear focus on the mission.

So, can leadership truly be selfless? In the purest sense,

probably not. But that's not the goal. The goal is to lead in a way that prioritizes the team while staying true to your own values and maintaining your ability to lead effectively. It's about balancing service with accountability, empathy with decision-making, and humility with strength.

To me, selfless leadership looks like this:

- **Listening First:** Take the time to understand your team's needs, challenges, and ideas before jumping to conclusions or solutions.

- **Empowering Others:** Giving your team the tools, trust, and autonomy they need to succeed, even if it means stepping out of the spotlight.

- **Setting Boundaries:** Knowing when to say "no" so you can focus on what truly matters and preserve your ability to lead effectively.

- **Being Transparent:** Sharing the reasoning behind decisions and admitting when you're wrong or uncertain.

- **Showing Empathy:** Recognizing the human side of leadership and making sure people feel seen, heard, and valued.

Leadership isn't about erasing yourself for the sake of others. It's about showing up fully, with integrity and purpose, to serve your team while staying grounded in who you are. True selflessness in leadership isn't about neglecting yourself—it's about using your strengths, energy, and vision to create an environment where everyone, including you, can thrive.

> Because at the end of the day, leadership isn't about you—
> it's about the impact you leave on those you lead.

Elevate Together: Why Your Success Is Incomplete Without Your Team

Mentorship and teamwork are not just buzzwords—they are foundational pillars for any leader seeking to pave a path of enduring success. In this engaging chapter, we delve into the practical aspects of building a culture where growth is not a solitary journey but a collective expedition. The essence of leadership transcends the boundaries of individual achievements to embrace the upliftment of every member within your sphere.

The Symbiosis of Mentorship

Imagine leadership as a two-way street. Here, the exchange of knowledge and experiences enriches both the mentor and the mentee. This relationship fosters an environment ripe for mutual growth, allowing leaders not only to impart wisdom but also to gain fresh perspectives. By prioritizing mentorship, you create a robust framework where learning is continuous and shared goals become attainable. This chapter will explore how nurturing these relationships can serve as a catalyst for team cohesion and individual development.

Team Dynamics: Harnessing Collective Strength

The dynamics of a team can often dictate its success or failure. Understanding how to effectively manage and participate in teams allows you to leverage the diverse skills and backgrounds of its members. We will look into strategies that enhance teamwork, promote healthy communication, and distribute leadership roles across the board. A leader's capability to orchestrate this harmony can transform ordinary groups into extraordinary ones, achieving more together than any individual could alone.

Leadership Strategies for an Empowering Ecosystem

True leadership is demonstrated not by how many followers you have but by how many leaders you create. In this section, we'll introduce practical strategies that help leaders foster an atmosphere where contribution and recognition go hand in hand. Encouraging your team members to take the initiative and acknowledge their achievements builds a positive feedback loop that enhances productivity and morale.

Through real-life examples and straightforward advice, this chapter aims to equip you with the tools necessary to cultivate an environment where everyone feels valued and empowered. By focusing on these elements, leaders can ensure that their journey towards success is not a lonely climb but a group ascent where every member feels invested in the collective outcome.

Remember, leadership is as much about paving the way forward as it is about ensuring no one is left behind. By adopting these principles, you set the stage for a legacy characterized not just by what you achieve but by how much you contribute to the growth of others around you.

In fostering this inclusive and supportive framework, we embrace a leadership model that enriches both the individual and the team—a model where every victory is shared and every challenge is met with collective resilience and intelligence.

As we navigate through these insights, let us commit to being leaders who don't just aim for the stars but bring their entire squad along for the journey. By doing so, we not only multiply our successes but also forge pathways for others to shine alongside us.

Creating an environment that fosters mutual growth is essential for effective leadership. When individuals feel supported, they are more likely to take risks, innovate, and contribute meaningfully to the team. Mentorship plays a crucial role in this process. By guiding others, sharing experiences, and offering constructive feedback, leaders can help cultivate talent within their teams. This not only benefits the mentees but also enhances the leader's own skills, creating a cycle of growth that benefits everyone involved.

At its core, mentorship is about *relationships*. It involves understanding the unique strengths and weaknesses of team members and providing tailored support to help them thrive. Leaders should actively seek opportunities to mentor others by engaging in open conversations about goals, aspirations, and challenges. This creates a safe space for team members to express their concerns and explore solutions collaboratively. Remember that *authenticity* is key; being genuine in your interactions fosters trust and encourages others to be open as well.

Support can take many forms. Sometimes, it's about offering encouragement during tough times or celebrating small victories along the way. Other times, it may involve challenging someone to step outside their comfort zone or facilitating connections with others who can help them grow professionally. Each interaction matters; even small gestures can significantly impact someone's confidence and motivation. Leaders should strive to be *accessible*, making themselves available for discussions and maintaining an open-door policy that invites dialogue.

Creating a culture of mutual growth also requires leaders to model vulnerability. Acknowledging one's own struggles and failures demonstrates that growth is a continuous journey rather than a destination. By sharing their experiences, leaders can inspire others to embrace their own challenges without fear of judgment. This kind of environment encourages learning from mistakes and viewing setbacks as opportunities for growth rather than obstacles.

Mentorship should not be a one-way street; it thrives on reciprocity. When leaders actively seek feedback from their team members, they reinforce the idea that everyone has something valuable to contribute. Encouraging individuals to share their perspectives not only strengthens relationships but also enhances decision-making processes within the team. Leaders who genuinely value input create a sense of ownership among team members, leading to greater engagement and commitment.

Recognizing achievements—both big and small—is another vital aspect of fostering mutual growth. Public acknowledgement of individual contributions can boost morale and motivate others to pursue excellence. However, it's equally important to celebrate collective successes. Highlighting how teamwork has led to positive outcomes reinforces the idea that success is often a group effort rather than solely individual achievement.

As we explore ways to nurture an environment where mentorship flourishes, remember that patience is essential. Building relationships takes time, and establishing trust cannot be rushed. Consistency in support will show your commitment to fostering growth among your team members, creating a lasting impact on their development.

Ready to unlock the dynamics of teamwork?

The Power of Team Dynamics

Understanding the dynamics of teamwork is crucial for any leader. **Teamwork is more than just assembling a group of people**; it involves creating an environment where individuals can thrive collectively. Each team member brings unique strengths, perspectives, and skills to the table. When harnessed effectively, these differences can lead to innovative solutions and improved outcomes. As a leader, recognizing and leveraging these individual contributions fosters a sense of belonging and purpose within the team.

Effective communication stands at the heart of any successful team. **Open dialogue encourages idea-sharing**, reduces misunderstandings, and builds trust. When team members feel free to express their thoughts, they are more likely to contribute creatively and collaboratively. A culture that promotes transparency allows individuals to voice concerns or challenges without fear of judgment. This openness not only strengthens relationships but also enhances problem-solving capabilities.

Moreover, **diversity within teams can significantly enhance collective achievement**. Diverse teams often outperform homogeneous ones because they approach problems from multiple angles. Different backgrounds bring varied experiences that can lead to richer discussions and innovative solutions. As a leader, actively seeking diverse perspectives can propel your team's effectiveness while fostering an inclusive atmosphere where everyone feels valued.

In addition to diversity, establishing clear roles and responsibilities is essential for maximizing teamwork. **When each member knows their specific contributions**, it reduces overlap and confusion, allowing the team to operate smoothly. Defining roles doesn't mean stifling creativity; rather, it provides a framework within which individuals can excel and collaborate effectively. Setting clear expectations ensures that everyone understands how their efforts align with the team's goals.

Another vital aspect of teamwork is mutual accountability. **When team members hold one another accountable**, they create a culture of responsibility that drives performance. This doesn't mean assigning blame when things go wrong; instead, it's about supporting each other in achieving shared objectives. Encouraging this mindset fosters a sense of ownership over both individual tasks and collective outcomes.

Celebrating successes together can further strengthen team bonds. **Acknowledging achievements—big or small—reinforces positive behaviour** and motivates team members to continue striving for excellence. Recognizing contributions publicly fosters morale and encourages others to step up as well. Acknowledgement serves as a powerful reminder that everyone's efforts matter in achieving shared goals.

Finally, effective leaders understand the importance of continuous learning within teams. **Encouraging growth through shared experiences can significantly enhance collective achievement**. This might involve regular feedback sessions, skill-sharing workshops, or collaborative problem-solving exercises. By fostering an environment where learning is prioritized, you create a resilient team ready to tackle future challenges together.

In summary, understanding teamwork dynamics is essential for young leaders navigating their roles. By focusing on communication, diversity, clarity in roles, accountability, recognition of achievements, and continuous learning, leaders can cultivate an environment where collective success flourishes. The journey toward effective teamwork begins with recognizing that every member's contribution plays a vital role in reaching common goals together.

Encouraging Contributions: The Heart of Leadership

Effective leadership is about more than directing tasks; it involves fostering a culture where everyone feels empowered to contribute. **Encouraging contribution begins with creating an environment where team members feel safe to share their ideas and perspectives.** This can be achieved by actively soliciting input during meetings and making a point to acknowledge and validate those contributions. When team members see that their voices matter, they are more likely to engage fully and offer valuable insights.

Building a platform for open communication is essential. **Make it a practice to invite feedback regularly, both in group settings and one-on-one interactions.** This not only enhances team dynamics but also provides leaders with diverse viewpoints that can lead to innovative solutions. When team members feel heard, they are more inclined to step outside their comfort zones and take initiative, knowing their efforts will be appreciated.

Recognition as a Motivator

Equally important is the role of recognition in motivating team members. **Acknowledging individual and collective achievements reinforces the idea that everyone's contributions are vital to the team's success.** A simple thank you or public acknowledgement during meetings can go a long way in boosting morale. Consider implementing a recognition program that highlights outstanding contributions regularly, whether through awards or shout-outs. This practice not only motivates those recognized but also inspires others to strive for excellence.

Recognition should be specific and timely. When a team member accomplishes something noteworthy, **address it immediately rather than waiting for a scheduled review period.** Highlighting specific actions taken or results achieved shows that you are paying attention and value their hard work. This approach fosters a sense of belonging and encourages ongoing effort toward collective goals.

Collaborative Decision-Making

Incorporating collaborative decision-making processes can also enhance contributions from all team members. **When team members**

participate in decision-making, they feel a sense of ownership over the outcomes, which can lead to increased commitment and accountability. Rather than making unilateral decisions, invite team input on significant choices affecting the group. This not only enriches the decision-making process with diverse perspectives but also builds trust within the team.

It's essential to set clear expectations when involving others in decisions. **Make sure everyone understands the parameters within which they can contribute, as well as how their input will be utilized.** This clarity helps prevent confusion while empowering individuals to share their insights confidently.

Balancing Leadership with Team Dynamics

A successful leader recognizes the balance between guiding the team and allowing space for individual contributions. **While it's crucial to provide direction, being overly directive can stifle creativity and limit engagement from your team members.** Strive for a balance where you offer guidance while simultaneously encouraging independence in thought and action.

To achieve this balance, assess your leadership style regularly. **Are you leaning too heavily on giving orders? Are you allowing enough room for your team's creativity?** By reflecting on these questions, you can adjust your approach as necessary, promoting an environment where everyone feels encouraged to innovate while still receiving the support they need.

Building Trust Through Transparency

Transparency is another critical factor in developing leadership strategies that encourage contribution and recognition within teams. **Being open about challenges, decisions, and successes fosters trust among team members, creating an atmosphere conducive to**

collaboration. Share not only victories but also struggles; this openness invites others to contribute ideas or solutions without fear of judgment.

Regular updates on project statuses or organizational changes help keep everyone informed and engaged in the process. **When people understand the bigger picture, they're more likely to invest themselves emotionally in their work**, leading to greater overall success for the team.

Cultivating a Growth Mindset

Finally, instilling a growth mindset within your team encourages continuous improvement and contribution from all members. **Promote an attitude that embraces challenges as opportunities for learning rather than obstacles to overcome.** Encourage experimentation, acknowledging that mistakes are part of growth rather than failures.

Fostering this mindset requires patience and consistent reinforcement from leaders. **Recognize efforts toward growth even if they don't always yield immediate success**, reinforcing that the journey matters just as much as the destination.

By implementing these strategies—encouraging contributions through open communication, recognizing achievements promptly, engaging in collaborative decision-making, balancing leadership styles with teamwork dynamics, maintaining transparency, and cultivating a growth mindset—you create an environment rich with potential for collective success. As leaders lift others through support and recognition, they also elevate themselves along with their teams toward shared goals.

As we wrap up our discussion, let's reflect on the transformative power of nurturing an environment where mentorship and teamwork are at the core. Leadership is not a solitary journey; it thrives on the collective energy and shared aspirations of a group. **Fostering mutual growth** isn't just a noble goal—it's a strategic move that amplifies success for all involved.

Consider the dynamic interplay within a team where each member is both a mentor and a mentee. This dual role enriches the learning experience, making the journey towards goals more inclusive and rewarding. It's about creating a culture where everyone feels valued and empowered to contribute their best. In such settings, the benefits of **collective achievement** become vividly apparent, not just in meeting targets but in the robust bonds formed along the way.

Developing leadership strategies that emphasize **contribution and recognition** is crucial. When team members see their efforts acknowledged, it fuels their motivation and commitment. It's akin to a gardener who tends to each plant with care, knowing that every individual growth adds to the beauty of the entire garden.

Remember, effective leadership is as much about elevating others as it is about ascending oneself. By encouraging and recognizing the contributions of each team member, you not only boost morale but also foster a sense of ownership and pride in the collective accomplishments.

As we move forward, let's carry with us the understanding that our success is deeply intertwined with the success of those we lead. By lifting as we climb, we don't just reach our goals—we multiply them, creating a legacy of leadership that resonates well beyond our immediate circle. Let this be the mindset as we navigate our route to success, ensuring that every mile travelled enriches not just us but also those who journey with us.

Chapter Thirteen

YOU TOOK THE L, NOW WHAT

How Does One Measure the Weight of Failure?

Failure has a way of sitting heavy on your shoulders, its weight shifting between shame, frustration, and reflection. I've carried that weight before, and I know it well. In leadership, where every decision has ripple effects, failure can feel personal. It can feel like your choices weren't enough, like you let your team down, or like you're at a standstill with no way forward. But over time, I've learned that the weight of failure isn't what defines you—it's what you do with it.

I remember one particularly painful experience early in my career. I had just taken on a leadership role in operations, and one of my first responsibilities was to oversee the rollout of a new process designed to streamline our workflow. On paper, it looked perfect—clear timelines, measurable goals, and seemingly flawless logic. I was confident.

But in practice, the rollout was a disaster. The process was too complex for the team to implement quickly, and we hadn't accounted for the nuances of how individual markets operated. The result? Missed deadlines, frustrated employees, and upset customers.

I still remember sitting in my office late at night, staring at the metrics that told the story of our failure. I felt every ounce of the weight. My first instinct was to blame external factors—things I couldn't control. But deep down, I knew that wouldn't help. If I wanted to move forward, I had to own what went wrong and figure out how to make it right.

The first step in measuring the weight of failure is *acknowledgement*. Too often, leaders try to downplay failures or shift the blame to save face. But failure, if ignored, has a way of festering and spreading. Instead of hiding from it, I sat down with my team and laid everything on the table.

"We missed the mark," I said. "Here's where I think we went wrong, but I want to hear from you. What could we have done differently?"

That conversation wasn't easy, but it was necessary. As my team shared their frustrations and insights, I realized that failure wasn't just about the outcome—it was about the missed opportunities along the way. We hadn't communicated clearly. We hadn't sought enough input. We hadn't tested the process thoroughly before rolling it out.

Once you've acknowledged failure, the next step is to *analyze*. This isn't about wallowing in what went wrong—it's about dissecting it, understanding it, and extracting lessons from it. For me, that meant diving into the feedback we'd received, revisiting our planning documents, and mapping out where the process had broken down.

What I found was humbling but enlightening. Our failure wasn't due to one catastrophic mistake; it was the result of small oversights that compounded over time. We hadn't prepared our team adequately. We hadn't built in enough flexibility. We had underestimated the learning curve.

By breaking the failure into its components, I was able to see it not as an insurmountable weight but as a series of missteps that could be corrected.

The final—and most important—step is *action*. Failure is only a dead end if you let it be. Once I understood what went wrong, I worked with my team to develop a revised plan. We simplified the process, implemented better training, and tested it in smaller markets before rolling it out network-wide.

The turnaround wasn't immediate, but it was significant. The second rollout was smoother, and the team felt more confident and supported. What had initially felt like a failure became a foundation for growth.

There's a metaphor I often think about when it comes to failure: ripples in a pond. Every action we take creates ripples, spreading outward in ways we can't always predict. When we fail, those ripples can feel overwhelming, like they'll disturb the entire pond forever. But over time, the water calms. The ripples fade. And what remains is the clarity of reflection—if we choose to see it.

Measuring the weight of failure isn't about how much it hurts—it's about how much you grow from it. It's about turning today's loss into tomorrow's lesson. To do that, I remind myself of three key principles:

1. **Own It:** Failure happens to everyone, but leaders have a responsibility to own their part in it. Acknowledging

failure doesn't diminish your authority—it strengthens it by showing accountability.

2. **Learn From It:** Every failure contains valuable lessons if you're willing to look for them. What went wrong? Why? What can you do differently next time? These questions are the starting point for improvement.

3. **Act on It:** Reflection without action is useless. Use what you've learned to create a better plan, process, or approach. Show your team that failure isn't the end—it's a step toward success.

Failure also has a way of humanizing us as leaders. It reminds us—and those we lead—that perfection isn't the goal. Progress is. I've found that some of the strongest bonds I've built with my teams have come from moments of shared failure. By owning my mistakes and involving them in the solution, I've earned the trust and respect that no victory could have achieved.

Looking back on that failed rollout, I don't feel the same weight I felt at the moment. Instead, I see it as a turning point—a chance to become a better leader. That's the thing about failure: it's not meant to define you. It's meant to refine you.

So, how do you measure the weight of failure? You don't. You measure what you do with it. Because, in the end, failure isn't about falling short—it's about rising stronger.

"Failure isn't about how far you fall; it's about how you rise, reflect, and rebuild. The weight of failure is measured not in mistakes but in the lessons you take forward." – Quentin J. Walker

When Victory Seems Lost: Embracing the Lessons of Failure

Leadership isn't just about steering through clear skies and calm waters; it's also about navigating storms. Failures, much like stormy weather, are inevitable. How you handle these setbacks can define your journey more significantly than your successes. This chapter delves into the indispensable skill of transforming losses into learning experiences. Here, we unpack the essence of **resilience**, analyze failures constructively, and foster a culture that not only tolerates but values insightful discussions about mistakes.

Building a Foundation with Resilience

Imagine resilience as a muscle that strengthens each time you push through a challenge. Leaders who cultivate this mindset don't see setbacks as roadblocks but as stepping stones to greater understanding and capability. This perspective shift is crucial, not just for individual growth but for inspiring your team. By embracing resilience, you set a precedent that failure is not a finale but an opportunity for growth.

Learning from the Lows

It's one thing to encourage bouncing back from failure; it's another to extract valuable lessons from it. This part of the journey involves a deep dive into what went wrong and why. The focus here isn't on assigning blame but on uncovering insights that prevent future mishaps. Developing strategies to effectively analyze failures equips you with foresight and prepares you better for future challenges.

Cultivating Openness and Insight

Leaders shape the environment in which their teams operate. By fostering an atmosphere where mistakes are openly discussed without fear of retribution, you encourage honesty and continuous improvement. Such an environment not only demystifies failure but also enhances collective learning and innovation within the team.

By considering these aspects, leaders can forge paths through their toughest times, turning potential defeats into defining victories. This process does not just preserve morale but actively boosts it, enhancing both leader and team performance in subsequent endeavours.

Navigating through failures with grace and acuity isn't just about salvaging lost situations; it's about setting a course for sustained success and innovation. As we delve deeper into these themes, remember that each setback faced with courage is not just another challenge overcome but a cornerstone laid for future triumphs.

This exploration isn't merely academic—it's a practical guide to mastering leadership resilience in the face of adversity. In the following sections, we'll dissect these ideas further, providing actionable strategies that can be applied directly to your leadership practices.

In leadership, embracing setbacks is crucial for personal and professional growth. **A resilient mindset** allows leaders to view failures not as dead ends but as valuable learning experiences. This perspective shift is essential for navigating the inevitable challenges that arise in any leadership role. Understanding that setbacks can lead to new insights and opportunities can transform how you approach obstacles.

Many people instinctively associate failure with negativity, often leading to feelings of inadequacy or fear of taking risks. However, this mindset can be counterproductive. Instead, consider every setback as a stepping stone toward improvement. For instance, after a project doesn't go as planned, reflect on what went wrong and what could have been done differently. This analysis is not just about identifying mistakes; it's about uncovering insights that can inform future decisions and strategies.

Cultivating resilience requires practice and intention. Start by re-framing your internal dialogue when faced with challenges. Instead of saying, *"I failed,"* try saying, *"I learned something important."* This simple shift can empower you to take ownership of your experiences rather than feeling defeated by them. Emphasizing growth over perfection fosters a healthier approach to leadership where experimentation and risk-taking are encouraged.

Moreover, surrounding yourself with supportive peers who also value resilience can amplify this mindset shift. Engaging in open discussions about failures—both yours and others'—can demystify the experience and normalize it within your team or organization. This creates an environment where learning from setbacks is seen as a collective journey rather than an individual burden.

When leaders exhibit resilience, they not only enhance their own capacity for growth but also inspire their teams to adopt the same attitude. **Modelling resilience** encourages team members to view challenges as opportunities for development rather than insurmountable problems. This shared perspective cultivates a culture of innovation where creativity thrives, knowing that mistakes are simply part of the process.

In addition to fostering resilience within yourself and your team, actively seeking feedback after setbacks is vital for continued growth. Constructive criticism can provide fresh perspectives that may not have been considered initially. By inviting input from others, you demonstrate humility and a genuine desire to improve, which further reinforces a resilient mindset.

Ultimately, adopting a resilient mindset positions you to navigate the complexities of leadership with confidence. It allows you to bounce back from difficulties stronger and more informed than before, paving the way for long-term success in your endeavours.

Ready to Explore Strategies for Learning from Failure?

Embrace the Lessons of Failure

Experiencing failure can be a painful reality for any leader, but understanding how to analyze those setbacks transforms them into powerful learning opportunities. **Recognizing failure as part of the growth process is essential.** When leaders face challenges, it's crucial to step back and assess what happened, why it happened, and how to prevent similar issues in the future. This self-reflection not only helps in personal development but also fosters a culture of continuous improvement within teams.

To effectively analyze failures, start by gathering data surrounding the event. **Look at all angles**: What were the circumstances leading up to the setback? What decisions were made? Who was involved? Collecting this information can provide clarity and context. It's essential to create an environment where team members feel comfortable sharing their perspectives without fear of blame. Encouraging open dialogue about failures can unveil insights that might otherwise remain hidden.

Identify Patterns and Trends

Once you have gathered relevant information, identify patterns or trends that may emerge from your analysis. **Ask yourself critical questions**: Are there recurring issues that need addressing? Do certain individuals or teams struggle more than others? By examining these patterns, you can pinpoint areas for improvement and develop targeted strategies to address them. This proactive approach not only mitigates future risks but also enhances your overall leadership effectiveness.

In addition to identifying trends, consider implementing a

structured framework for analyzing failures. A common method is the "5 Whys," where you ask "why" multiple times until you reach the root cause of an issue. This technique promotes deeper understanding rather than simply addressing surface-level symptoms. By drilling down into the fundamental reasons behind a failure, you empower yourself and your team to implement meaningful changes.

Create Actionable Plans

After identifying root causes and patterns, it's time to create actionable plans for improvement. **Set specific goals** that are achievable and measurable. For instance, if communication breakdown was a factor in a project's failure, develop strategies to enhance team communication channels or establish regular check-ins. Assign responsibilities clearly so everyone knows their role in the plan moving forward.

Moreover, ensure these plans include checkpoints for revisiting progress and making adjustments as necessary. Regularly assessing how well you're implementing these changes keeps everyone accountable and focused on continuous improvement.

Foster a Growth Mindset

A key element in learning from failures is fostering a growth mindset within your team. Encourage your team members to view challenges as chances for personal development rather than setbacks. **Promote a culture where feedback is constructive**, focusing on behaviours and outcomes rather than personal attributes. Celebrate small wins along with lessons learned from failures; this balance helps maintain morale while reinforcing the value of resilience.

By modelling this growth mindset yourself—showing vulnerability when things don't go as planned—you set an example for others to follow. When leaders openly discuss their experiences with failure, it normalizes these challenges and opens doors for candid conversations about improvement.

Document and Share Insights

Lastly, documenting lessons learned from each failure creates an invaluable resource over time. Consider creating a shared repository where insights can be recorded and accessed by team members easily. This practice not only reinforces accountability but also builds a collective knowledge base that everyone can draw from in future endeavours.

Sharing these insights during team meetings or workshops further solidifies understanding within your group. When individuals see how past failures have contributed to current successes, they become more engaged in their work and motivated to learn continuously.

In summary, developing strategies to analyze and learn from failures is vital in cultivating resilience as a leader. By embracing setbacks as teaching moments rather than obstacles, you create an environment ripe for growth—not just for yourself but also for your entire team. The journey toward success is rarely linear; it's filled with twists and turns that require reflection, adaptation, and, above all, a commitment to learning from every experience along the way.

Fostering Open Dialogue About Mistakes

Creating an environment where mistakes can be openly discussed is essential for any leader looking to foster growth within their team. When leaders encourage a culture of transparency, they empower team members to share their experiences without the fear of judgment. This openness not only promotes trust but also facilitates collective learning. **When team members feel safe to admit their missteps, they are more likely to engage in constructive conversations that lead to solutions.**

A significant barrier to this kind of culture often stems from a fear of repercussions. Many individuals worry that admitting a mistake might lead to negative evaluations or job insecurity. As a leader, it's crucial to actively dismantle these fears by modelling vulnerability yourself. Share your own setbacks and the lessons you've learned from them. **When leaders demonstrate that they can own their mistakes without shame, it sends a powerful message that errors are a natural part of the learning process.**

To further cultivate this culture, consider implementing regular "failure debriefs" or "learning circles." These meetings can serve as dedicated spaces where team members reflect on recent challenges and discuss what went wrong and how things could be improved. Encourage open dialogue by asking probing questions that guide the conversation toward constructive outcomes. For instance, instead of simply asking what went wrong, pose questions like, *"What could we have done differently?"* or *"What valuable insights have we gained from this experience?"*

Another effective approach is to celebrate the lessons learned from mistakes rather than just focusing on the failures themselves. Acknowledge the courage it takes to admit when things haven't gone as planned. **By celebrating these moments, you reinforce the idea that learning is an ongoing journey—one that requires humility and resilience.** This shift in perspective can transform how your team views failure, turning it into a stepping stone rather than a stumbling block.

Moreover, fostering a culture of open discussion around mistakes can lead to innovation. When team members feel comfortable sharing their failures, new ideas often emerge from these conversations. They may uncover previously unconsidered solutions or strategies that could benefit the entire team or organization. **Encouraging this kind of dialogue not only enhances problem-solving abilities but also**

strengthens collaboration among team members.

It's also important for leaders to provide constructive feedback when discussing mistakes. Instead of focusing solely on what went wrong, frame your feedback in a way that highlights potential improvements and future actions. **This approach helps individuals feel supported and understood rather than criticized**, which in turn fosters greater commitment to personal growth.

Finally, remember that establishing such a culture takes time and persistence. It's not enough to simply state that mistakes are welcome; you must continually demonstrate this through your actions and words. Regularly check in with your team about their comfort levels in discussing failures and make adjustments based on their feedback.

As you work toward cultivating an environment where mistakes are openly discussed and viewed as opportunities for growth, you will empower your team to embrace challenges confidently and develop resilience together. This shift will not only enhance individual capabilities but will also contribute significantly to overall team success and cohesion moving forward.

As we navigate the journey of leadership, it's crucial to acknowledge that not all roads will be smooth. The true test comes not from the victories we celebrate but from how we handle the setbacks. Embracing failures as stepping stones rather than stumbling blocks can profoundly shape our path forward.

Cultivating a resilient mindset is more than just bouncing back; it's about seeing every setback as a setup for a comeback. Think of it as being in a laboratory where each experiment, successful or not, teaches us something valuable. This mindset doesn't just happen overnight. It requires practice, patience, and persistence. Encourage yourself and your team to view each challenge as an opportunity to learn and grow.

When it comes to **developing strategies to analyze and learn from failures**, the approach is straightforward but impactful. Dive deep into what went wrong without pointing fingers. Analyze the situation with a clear head and a focus on solutions. What can be done better next time? What have we learned about our team and ourselves through this process? This kind of analysis is invaluable because it turns every misstep into a lesson that paves the way for future success.

Furthermore, fostering an environment where **mistakes are discussed openly and constructively** is essential for any thriving organization. When team members feel safe to express their concerns and share their failures, it not only strengthens the bonds within the team but also propels innovation. People are less afraid to take risks when they know their team views mistakes as necessary for growth.

Each of these strategies not only helps in overcoming the challenges but also in embedding valuable lessons into the fabric of our leadership style. By transforming our approach to setbacks, we not only enhance our own resilience but also inspire those around us to navigate their paths with courage and confidence.

Remember, every leader will face setbacks. The difference lies in how they respond. By viewing these moments through a lens of learning and growth, you set yourself—and your team—up for long-term success. Let's carry these insights forward, using them as tools to build a more robust, more resilient leadership journey.

Chapter Fourteen

NO SHORTCUTS, JUST HUSTLE

Who is on the Grill?

There's something special about BBQ. The slow sizzle of meat, the smoky aroma wafting through the air, and the satisfaction of seeing it all come together—it's a process that demands patience, precision, and, most importantly, hustle. What most people don't realize is that great BBQ is as much about managing the fire as it is about the food. Too hot, and you burn everything. Too low, and you'll never get it done. It's a balancing act, and when you're the one manning the grill, the responsibility is all on you.

Leadership feels a lot like tending a grill. It's about being in control of the heat, knowing when to turn things up and when to let them simmer. And when the heat is on—whether it's a high-pressure situation at work or a crowded backyard full of hungry guests—you've got to be ready to step up, take charge, and deliver.

I think back to one of the toughest challenges I faced in my career. We were launching a new process to improve operational efficiency, and from the outset, it felt like a fire that wouldn't stay lit. Nothing was going smoothly. Team members were frustrated, deadlines were slipping, and complaints were piling up from customers.

It reminded me of a BBQ gone wrong—when the coals won't catch, the meat isn't cooking evenly, and people are circling the grill asking, "How much longer?" You've got to figure it out fast, or you'll lose everyone's confidence.

The first thing I did was take a step back and assess the situation. Just like tending the grill, you can't rush into adjustments without understanding what's really going on. Was the process broken, or was it a matter of execution? Were we missing resources, or were we just misaligned on priorities?

I realized the issue wasn't with the process itself—it was with how we were communicating it. The team didn't fully understand their roles, and the lack of clarity was creating unnecessary friction. It was like trying to grill without knowing the temperature—you're bound to get uneven results.

I called the team together for an honest conversation. "Here's the deal," I said. "We're off track, but this isn't about pointing fingers. Let's figure out what's not working and how we're going to fix it."

Much like adjusting the grill's airflow to get the heat just right, we started fine-tuning our approach. I broke the process into smaller, more manageable steps, assigned clear responsibilities, and set up regular check-ins to make sure we stayed aligned.

The second thing I did was get my hands dirty—literally and figuratively. Just like BBQ, where you can't be afraid to flip the meat yourself or adjust the coals, leadership during a crisis means being in the thick of it with your team.

I made it a point to be on the floor with them, answering questions, troubleshooting issues, and finding solutions in real time. When one team member was struggling to meet a deadline, I sat down with them to figure out what was getting in the way. We adjusted their workload and brought in extra support, ensuring they could succeed without burning out.

It wasn't glamorous, but it was necessary. When the heat is on, your team needs to know you're in it with them, working just as hard to make sure everything turns out right.

Finally, I focused on the end goal. In BBQ, the result is what everyone remembers—how the food tastes, how it's presented, and whether everyone leaves satisfied. The same is true in leadership. No one cares how many fires you put out along the way if the end result isn't worth it.

I kept reminding the team why this process mattered. It wasn't just about hitting a target or meeting a deadline—it was about setting us up for long-term success. By keeping the big picture in focus, we were able to push through the challenges and deliver something we could all be proud of.

When I think about leadership, I often think about BBQ. It's not just about the food—it's about the care, the hustle, and the effort you put into making it great. You can't cut corners, and you can't rush it. Whether you're grilling ribs for a family gathering or leading a team through a tough time, the same principles apply:

1. **Set the Foundation:** Just like lighting the coals, you need a strong foundation. Make sure your team has clear

goals, roles, and resources.

2. **Adjust as Needed:** When the heat isn't right, adjust. Listen to feedback, analyze what's not working, and adapt your approach.

3. **Be Present:** Great BBQ and great leadership both require attention. Stay involved, stay engaged, and show your team that you're in it with them.

4. **Focus on the Outcome:** Never lose sight of the end goal. Whether it's a perfectly smoked brisket or a successful project launch, keep everyone aligned on what you're working toward.

Leadership, like BBQ, isn't about shortcuts. It's about putting in the time, paying attention to the details, and staying committed, even when the heat is on. And when you get it right, there's nothing more satisfying than seeing the results of your hard work and knowing you gave it your all.

So, who tends the grill when the heat is on? The leader who's ready to hustle, adapt, and deliver—no matter how hot it gets.

Are You Steering or Just Along for the Ride?

Navigating the complexities of leadership can sometimes feel like trying to find your way through an intricate maze. Yet, the essence of true leadership lies in *having a clear vision* and steering not just oneself but also one's team towards that goal with unwavering determination. As we delve into this chapter, we focus on the **indispensable role of diligence, consistency, and hard work** in crafting successful leadership.

The journey of leadership is relentless and demands more than occasional bursts of effort; it requires a sustained, robust work ethic. As you've advanced through the previous chapters, gathering insights on accountability, decision-making, self-awareness, and team-building, we now reach a pivotal moment. This chapter aims to reinforce the necessity of embedding these skills deeply into your daily leadership practice.

The Foundation of Hard Work

Every seasoned leader knows that there are no shortcuts to real success. The path to achieving and sustaining leadership excellence is paved with the tough stones of **hard work and persistence**. Here, we explore how to lay down a strong foundation based on a solid work ethic. It's about doing the small things right every single day, which accumulate over time to produce remarkable results.

Leadership isn't merely about setting directions; it's profoundly about how you accompany your team along that path, how you inspire them during challenges, and how you keep them aligned with the core objectives. We will discuss methods that help establish these practices not as forced efforts but as natural elements of your leadership style.

Consistency is King

In the realm of effective leadership, consistency acts like gravity: it holds everything together. Without it, no amount of talent or opportunity can lead you to maintain success. We'll examine strategies to enhance your consistency in leadership tasks, which will ensure that your team trusts your vision and follows you willingly.

Persistence in refining these leadership traits can often be challenging; however, it demands a commitment to continuous improvement and learning. As we have seen throughout this book, mastering key leadership skills does not happen overnight, nor does it happen by chance—it happens by choice.

Steadfast Leadership

Encouraging persistent excellence involves nurturing an environment where every team member feels valued and understands their role in the larger picture. This chapter emphasizes not only setting high standards but also consistently upholding them, thereby fostering an atmosphere of excellence within your team.

This pursuit requires embracing both successes and setbacks as opportunities for growth. By maintaining focus on long-term goals while managing day-to-day responsibilities, you demonstrate to your team that every step—no matter how small—is crucial towards achieving overarching objectives.

As we prepare to conclude our journey through this book, remember that the principles discussed are not merely theoretical but are actionable tactics that have been tried and tested across many leadership scenarios. They are designed to equip you with **confidence** and **clarity**, turning potential into performance.

By understanding and implementing these lessons, you'll be better prepared to steer your career with purpose and precision—transforming challenges into stepping stones for success. This chapter is about empowering you with knowledge but also inspiring you to act upon it diligently as you continue navigating your route to effective leadership.

Leadership is not a title; it's a commitment to hard work and relentless effort. At the core of effective leadership lies **diligence**, **consistency**, and **hard work**. These qualities are not just buzzwords—they are the foundational blocks upon which successful leadership is built. When leaders embrace these principles, they foster an environment where both they and their teams can thrive. It's essential to recognize that there are no shortcuts in this journey; progress comes from sustained effort and determination.

Diligence is more than merely showing up; it's about fully engaging with your responsibilities every single day. A diligent leader demonstrates reliability, which in turn inspires trust among team members. When you consistently put in the effort, your team will notice. They'll see that you're committed to the cause, and this can motivate them to adopt a similar mindset. As you embody diligence, you create a culture that values hard work, encouraging everyone to step up their game.

Consistency is another critical aspect of successful leadership. It means being dependable—not just in your actions but also in your decision-making. When you make choices based on well-thought-out principles rather than whims, your team learns to rely on you. This fosters a sense of security and stability within the group. **Being consistent helps avoid confusion** and miscommunication, as team members understand what to expect from you as their leader.

Hard work cannot be overstated. It requires putting in the hours and effort even when motivation wanes or challenges arise. A leader who is willing to roll up their sleeves sets a powerful example for the team. They show that achieving goals takes more than just desire; it necessitates dedication and resilience. This attitude can be contagious, prompting others to adopt a similar approach toward their tasks.

The path of leadership is often fraught with obstacles, but how a leader responds to these challenges speaks volumes about their character. Leaders who tackle difficulties with grit reinforce the idea that hard work pays off in the long run. They become a source of inspiration for their teams, demonstrating that perseverance leads to growth—both personally and professionally.

Moreover, success doesn't happen overnight; it's usually the result of countless small efforts accumulated over time. Every task completed diligently contributes to larger goals being met. Celebrate these small victories with your team; recognizing progress along the way keeps morale high and emphasizes the importance of consistent hard work.

As young leaders navigate new roles or ventures, they might feel overwhelmed by expectations or unsure of how to lead effectively. The key takeaway here is simple: committing to diligence, consistency, and hard work lays the groundwork for successful leadership. These traits not only enhance personal growth but also cultivate a thriving team dynamic where everyone strives for excellence together.

Are You Ready to Build Your Leadership Foundation?

Establishing a Strong Work Ethic

A strong work ethic is the bedrock of effective leadership. It's not just about putting in hours; it's about the quality and intention behind those hours. **Diligence, consistency, and hard work** are crucial elements that define a leader's journey. When you commit to these principles, you set a powerful example for your team, creating an environment where everyone feels motivated to contribute their best efforts. The challenge lies in developing this work ethic and ensuring it becomes ingrained in your daily routine.

To cultivate a robust work ethic, start by setting clear expectations for yourself. Define what success looks like in your role and outline the steps necessary to achieve it. This clarity will help you stay focused and accountable. For example, if your goal is to improve team performance, break it down into actionable tasks—such as regular check-ins with team members or implementing new training programs. **By establishing specific objectives**, you create a roadmap that guides your actions and decisions.

Another vital aspect of building a strong work ethic is embracing discipline. Discipline isn't merely about adhering to rules; it's about developing habits that support your goals. Create a daily schedule that allocates time for high-priority tasks and stick to it as closely as possible. This structure helps you maintain focus and prevents procrastination from derailing your progress. *Over time, these small daily commitments accumulate*, leading to significant achievements.

Equally important is fostering an environment of accountability within your team. Encourage open communication where team members feel comfortable discussing their challenges and progress. This openness creates a culture where everyone understands the importance of diligence and feels responsible for their contributions. When team members see each other working hard toward shared goals, they are more likely to rise to the occasion themselves.

Remember that setbacks are part of any leadership journey. How you respond to them can significantly impact your work ethic and that of your team. Instead of viewing failures as reasons to give up, use them as learning opportunities. Reflect on what went wrong, make adjustments, and move forward with renewed determination. **Resilience in the face of challenges** not only strengthens your own work ethic but also inspires those around you to persevere.

Additionally, prioritize self-care as part of building a strong work ethic. It might seem counterintuitive, but taking care of yourself can enhance your productivity and focus. Make time for breaks during the day to recharge mentally and physically. Engaging in activities outside of work—such as exercise or hobbies—can provide fresh perspectives and boost creativity when you're back at the helm.

Lastly, seek regular feedback from peers and mentors on your performance and commitment levels. Constructive criticism can be invaluable for identifying areas where you can improve or adjust your approach to work more effectively. *Embrace feedback* as an opportunity for growth rather than something negative; it's essential for refining your leadership skills.

By consciously implementing these methods into your daily routine, you can establish a strong foundational work ethic that will serve you well throughout your leadership career. Your commitment to diligence, consistency, and hard work will not only elevate your performance but also inspire those around you to strive for excellence together with you on this path forward.

The Value of Persistence

Persistence is a cornerstone of effective leadership. In a world that often seeks quick results and instant gratification, the ability to stay committed to long-term goals stands out. Leaders must understand that challenges will arise and setbacks are inevitable. The key lies in how one responds to these hurdles. Instead of viewing obstacles as roadblocks, they should be seen as opportunities for growth and learning. This shift in perspective not only enhances resilience but also inspires the team to adopt a similar mindset.

Developing a culture of persistence within a team is crucial. When leaders demonstrate unwavering determination, it sets a standard for everyone involved. **Showing commitment during tough times can galvanize a group**, fostering an environment where challenges are met with collective resolve rather than frustration. Encourage team members to voice their concerns and struggles; acknowledging these feelings can lead to innovative solutions and stronger collaboration.

The Pursuit of Excellence

Striving for excellence isn't about perfection; it's about consistent improvement. Leaders must champion this pursuit by setting clear performance standards and encouraging their teams to reach beyond their comfort zones. **This involves celebrating small wins** as much as major achievements. Recognizing incremental progress helps build momentum and reinforces the idea that every step counts on the path to success.

In practical terms, leaders can implement regular feedback loops. These sessions create an open dialogue about performance and expectations, allowing for continuous adjustment and refinement of goals. When feedback is framed positively, it becomes a tool for motivation rather than criticism. This encourages team members to take ownership of their development while also reinforcing the importance of persistent effort.

Embracing Challenges

Challenges are not just obstacles; they are essential components of growth. Leaders should embrace difficult situations as chances to learn and adapt. It's important to communicate this philosophy to the team, emphasizing that overcoming challenges often leads to greater capabilities and confidence. **When leaders share stories of their own struggles**, it humanizes them and reinforces the idea that perseverance is part of the journey.

Moreover, cultivating a problem-solving mindset among team members can significantly enhance their ability to face challenges head-on. Encourage brainstorming sessions where all ideas are welcomed, fostering creativity in finding solutions. This not only empowers individuals but also strengthens teamwork as they collaborate towards common goals.

Building Confidence Through Consistency

Confidence in leadership grows from consistent actions over time. By demonstrating reliability—through follow-through on commitments and maintaining high standards—leaders instil trust within their teams. This trust is crucial when navigating through uncertain times or pursuing ambitious objectives. **When team members believe in their leader's dedication**, they are more likely to mirror that commitment in their work.

To build this consistency, leaders should establish routines that promote accountability both for themselves and their teams. Regular check-ins on progress not only keep everyone aligned but also reinforce the notion that persistence pays off in achieving excellence.

Maintaining Focus Amid Distractions

In today's fast-paced environment, distractions abound, often pulling focus away from essential tasks. Leaders need to help their teams maintain clarity on priorities amidst this chaos. Setting clear objectives provides direction; however, it's equally important to regularly revisit these goals together as a team.

Encourage reflection on what truly matters within daily tasks and projects. This practice can help individuals identify time-wasting activities that hinder progress toward excellence, reinforcing the importance of prioritization in achieving long-term success.

Celebrating Progress

Recognizing progress is vital in sustaining motivation over time. Leaders should make it a point to celebrate achievements—both big and small—within the team's journey toward its goals. This acknowledgement serves as a powerful reminder that persistence leads to results.

Create opportunities for recognition during meetings or through internal communications platforms where accomplishments can be highlighted publicly. Celebrating milestones fosters a sense of community within the team, reinforcing collective effort towards shared objectives.

Through persistence and an unwavering focus on excellence, leaders cultivate an environment where both individuals and teams thrive despite the challenges ahead. As these principles become embedded in everyday practices, young leaders will find themselves better equipped to navigate the complexities of leadership with confidence and purpose.

As we draw the threads of this discourse together, let's reflect on the journey we've undertaken. Leadership is not merely about occupying a position; it's about action and **diligent, consistent action** at that. To steer a team effectively towards success, it's essential to cultivate a robust work ethic that marries hard work with persistence. These qualities are not just beneficial but necessary in the toolkit of any aspiring leader.

The essence of leadership lies in the ability to maintain a clear vision and to communicate this effectively to your team. It's about *showing up*, day in and day out, and demonstrating through your actions how each piece of the puzzle fits together to create a larger picture of success. **Establishing a strong foundational work ethic** isn't just about working hard; it's about working smart—identifying priorities, delegating effectively, and always aligning with the core objectives of your team.

Moreover, the pursuit of excellence is a continuous journey. It doesn't end with achieving one goal or milestone; rather, it's about setting new benchmarks and striving for them with unwavering commitment. This **steadfast pursuit** is what distinguishes a leader from a follower. Excellence in leadership requires not just setting the bar high but consistently ensuring that every action and decision helps in reaching and raising that bar.

Throughout this book, we've tackled the core issues that you, as a young leader, might face—from mastering the art of decision-making to building accountable teams and enhancing self-awareness. Each chapter has built upon the last, providing you with a practical roadmap designed from real-life experiences and timeless lessons. The goal has always been clear: to equip you with the confidence and skills necessary to navigate your leadership path with purpose and clarity.

Remember, the journey of leadership is as rewarding as it is challenging. It demands more than just knowledge—it requires application, adaptation, and, above all, an unwavering commitment to growth. As you move forward, take these lessons not just as guidelines but as companions on your journey to becoming a leader who not only leads but inspires.

Let these insights be your guide as you continue to drive forward, steering your team towards success with clarity and determination. The road might be long and demanding, but remember, there are no shortcuts—just hustle.

EPILOGUE

Journey's End: Your Pathway to Leadership Mastery

As we close the pages on this exploration of leadership through the lens of Route 17, take a moment to reflect on how far we've travelled together. Leadership is not a destination; it's a continuous journey of growth, resilience, and purpose. Through these chapters, we've navigated the terrain of accountability, decision-making, self-awareness, and team-building—each a vital marker along the road to effective leadership.

Route 17, for me, was more than a childhood bus ride—it was a classroom. Each stop, each fare counted out, and every observation of the people around me taught lessons that have guided my leadership journey. In the same way, I hope this book has equipped you to identify and embrace your own formative moments, turning them into actionable leadership insights.

Leadership isn't theoretical; it lives in action. Perhaps you're already envisioning how to apply these lessons in your life. Consider implementing enhanced accountability within your team by introducing transparent goals and regular follow-ups. Imagine using self-awareness to navigate the challenges of a high-stakes project, identifying how your strengths and growth areas impact your team's performance. These are not just concepts—they're tools waiting to be used.

Take, for example, the importance of reflection. Maintaining a journal to document your thoughts, successes, and failures isn't just an exercise; it's a strategy. It allows you to see patterns in your behavior, learn from them, and refine your approach. Similarly, initiating regular feedback sessions with your team or peers fosters accountability and ensures alignment with shared goals.

Each chapter of this book is a building block, but it's up to you to construct something meaningful with them. Leadership isn't a one-size-fits-all solution; it's deeply personal shaped by your experiences, values, and aspirations. The real challenge lies in translating these lessons from words into deeds.

For instance, think about decision-making. In today's fast-paced environment, leaders often feel pressured to make decisions quickly, sometimes at the expense of thorough consideration. What if you paused, applied the frameworks we discussed, and made choices that balanced immediate needs with long-term impact?

Or consider the chapter on building the right team. Are you ensuring that every member of your team brings value not just in skills but in energy, attitude, and alignment with your vision? Leadership is about people, and one of your most significant responsibilities is ensuring that the right people are on the bus with you.

While this book has covered a lot of ground, it's important to remember that leadership is a lifelong pursuit. There's always more to learn, adapt to, and master. As you move forward, consider diving deeper into areas like cultural influences on leadership styles, managing remote teams, or navigating generational differences in the workplace. These are dynamic aspects of leadership that will continue to evolve, requiring you to stay curious and adaptive.

But even as you seek new knowledge, never lose sight of the fundamentals. Accountability, self-awareness, communication, and resilience are timeless principles. They are the foundation on which all great leadership is built.

This journey has been about more than just teaching principles—

it's been about empowerment. The true measure of leadership isn't what you know; it's what you do with what you know. Every decision you make every action you take, has the potential to inspire others, create change, and leave a lasting impact.

As you prepare to take these lessons into your own life, remember that the road ahead won't always be smooth. There will be detours, obstacles, and moments of doubt. But leadership isn't about avoiding challenges—it's about rising to meet them. It's about keeping your eyes on the horizon, even when the path feels uncertain.

I leave you with this thought, one that has guided me throughout my journey: Leadership is not about perfection; it's about progress. It's about showing up every day with the intention to learn, grow, and lead with purpose.

John C. Maxwell said it best: "A leader is one who knows the way, goes the way, and shows the way." My hope is that this book has served as a compass, guiding you toward not just knowing the way but confidently travelling it and inspiring others to follow.

Now, it's your turn to step up, take the wheel, and lead with courage, clarity, and compassion. The journey continues, and I can't wait to see where it takes you.